Simulation with Python

Develop Simulation and Modeling in Natural Sciences, Engineering, and Social Sciences

Rongpeng Li
Aiichiro Nakano

Apress®

Simulation with Python: Develop Simulation and Modeling in Natural Sciences, Engineering, and Social Sciences

Rongpeng Li
Los Angeles, CA, USA

Aiichiro Nakano
Los Angeles, CA, USA

ISBN-13 (pbk): 978-1-4842-8184-0
https://doi.org/10.1007/978-1-4842-8185-7

ISBN-13 (electronic): 978-1-4842-8185-7

Managing Director, Apress Media LLC: Welmoed Spahr
Acquisitions Editor: Celestin Suresh John
Development Editor: Laura Berendson
Coordinating Editor: Aditee Mirashi

Cover designed by eStudioCalamar

Cover image designed by Freepik (www.freepik.com)

Distributed to the book trade worldwide by Springer Science+Business Media New York, 1 New York Plaza, Suite 4600, New York, NY 10004-1562, USA. Phone 1-800-SPRINGER, fax (201) 348-4505, e-mail orders-ny@ springer-sbm.com, or visit www.springeronline.com. Apress Media, LLC is a California LLC and the sole member (owner) is Springer Science + Business Media Finance Inc (SSBM Finance Inc). SSBM Finance Inc is a **Delaware** corporation.

For information on translations, please e-mail booktranslations@springernature.com; for reprint, paperback, or audio rights, please e-mail bookpermissions@springernature.com.

Apress titles may be purchased in bulk for academic, corporate, or promotional use. eBook versions and licenses are also available for most titles. For more information, reference our Print and eBook Bulk Sales web page at http://www.apress.com/bulk-sales.

Any source code or other supplementary material referenced by the author in this book is available to readers on GitHub (Github.com/apress). For more detailed information, please visit http://www.apress. com/source-code.

Printed on acid-free paper

To Yan, for everything.

—Ron

Table of Contents

About the Authors

 **Rongpeng Li** is the business intelligence team lead at Unit21. He was a senior data scientist and data science instructor at Unit21. Rongpeng Li graduated from USC with two masters, one in physics and another in electrical engineering. He is a keen educator. He authored one statistics book derived from his voluntary services in the data community.

 **Aiichiro Nakano** (advisory author) is a professor of computer science and physics and astronomy with joint appointments in quantitative and computational biology and collaboratory for advanced computing and simulations at the University of Southern California. He received a PhD in physics from the University of Tokyo, Japan. His research areas are scalable scientific algorithms, high-end parallel supercomputing, scientific visualization and informatics, and computational materials science. He is a Fellow of the American Physical Society.

About the Technical Reviewer

 **Kacie Webster** is currently a data analyst in the telecommunications industry. After graduating from San Diego State University with a degree in statistics and economics, she completed a data science bootcamp where she gained the skills to become a data professional. As Kacie continues her journey, she enjoys the constant growth and change that comes with the data world.

Acknowledgments

Rongpeng Li would like to thank all his previous students for the inspiration of this book, from readers at local libraries to learners in his Zoom classroom.

Introduction

This book is a small gift to a younger me, probably in high school or even earlier. This book is by no means written for seasoned researchers or professionals. It should be treated as the first bite of ice cream which makes you want more.

This book contains several scientific simulation topics, ranging from physics, biology, and even finance. The approach is very gentle and newcomer friendly. I tried to remove the majority of the complexity that I would learn with the knowledge and scientific training I already had. Instead, I did my best to keep the most important essence in each topic. The persona in my mind is a young and curious student who just got the first computer and learned some basic programming, probably from the older brother. This student, pictured as a younger me, would be able to follow the content of this book without any difficulty and get amazed by the beautiful visualizations and scientific conclusions.

Each topic in this book is rather independent. According to the level of technical difficulty and required background knowledge, I categorize the chapters into three groups. Readers can start with any chapter.

Easy:

Chapter 1: Calculating Pi with Monte Carlo Simulation

Chapter 4: Balls in a 2-D Box, a Simple Physics Engine

Medium:

Chapter 2: Markov Chain, a Peek into the Future

Chapter 3: Multi-armed Bandits, Probability Simulation, and Bayesian Statistics

Chapter 7: Rock, Scissors, and Paper: Multi-agent Simulation

Chapter 8: Disease Spreading, Simulating COVID-19 Outbreak

Chapter 9: Misinformation Spreading and Simulations on a Graph

Hard:

Chapter 5: Percolation, Threshold, and Phase Change

Chapter 6: Queuing System: How Stock Trades Are Made

I hope you enjoy this book as much as I do.

## CHAPTER 1

Calculating Pi with Monte Carlo Simulation

Background

When Stanislaw Ulam, a Polish-American mathematician and nuclear physicist, invented and formulated the modern Monte Carlo method in the 1940s, he and his colleagues named the method Monte Carlo because Ulam's uncle often borrowed his relatives' money to gamble in Monaco's Monte Carlo Casino. Stanislaw Ulam and many other brilliant scientists were working on the secret nuclear weapon program now known as the Manhattan Project. The Monte Carlo method was programmed to simulate nuclear reactions. To some degree, the Monte Carlo method helped shape the world we see today.

Before theorems or algorithms take their formal names in academics, they often have been studied by curious pioneers using fun, example-based approaches. Let's start with a story.

The Wise Persons' Competition

Suppose one day in the 1500s, somewhere in the Middle East, a king gave 24 hours to the two wisest persons, including you, in his kingdom to calculate the value of π in the most elegant way. The king generously promised any reasonable resources you want.

π is the ratio of the perimeter and the diameter of a circle. Oftentimes, we also call the perimeter of a circle circumference denoted with the letter C. The quantities are illustrated in Figure 1-1.

© Rongpeng Li and Aiichiro Nakano 2022
R. Li and A. Nakano, *Simulation with Python*, https://doi.org/10.1007/978-1-4842-8185-7_1

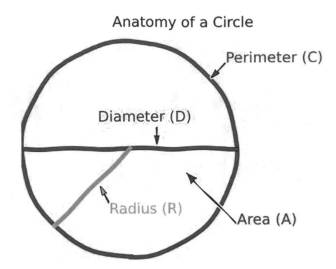

Figure 1-1. *Notations for a circle*

Your opponent asked for the finest papers, strings, and rulers in the kingdom. He started partitioning the circle immediately after the king announced the contest. His approach was the same as the method that a Chinese mathematician *Chongzhi Zu* used about 1000 years ago.

Well, as in the 16th century, calculus was not invented. What were you going to do, wise person? You were not sitting there and letting your opponent win! Instead, you asked the king for 1000 persons to help you with the calculation. You also asked for enough fine sand grains, regular papers of size 10 inch by 10 inch, rulers, and strings. The king generously approved your request with curiosity.

Estimating Pi by Sprinkling Grains

Now, you have 1000 men standing in line at your command. This is what you are going to do. You asked each of them to draw the biggest circle inside the square paper. After that, they were required to *randomly* sprinkle *1000* sand grains on the paper. Each person was required to count carefully and record the number of grains inside the circle. Of course, the grains might accidently fall outside of the paper. In that case, the person was required to resprinkle until all 1000 grains were on the paper.

The king was puzzled. You looked confident because you knew your king was not a super math person, just like most readers of this book, and easily got bored with plain equations. Your opponent had a lot of geometrical gibberish to explain to the king.

Your opponent was using polygons' perimeters to approximate the circle. As you can see from Figure 1-2, the sectioning of the perimeter became visibly tedious as the number of edges grew.

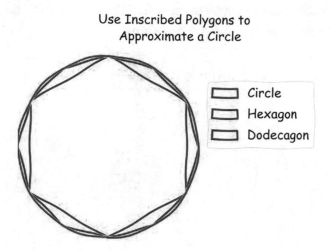

Figure 1-2. *Use polygons to approximate a circle*

You noticed your opponent would always get a value lower than the true perimeter because the polygons were inscribed, which means they were always inside the circle. In order to get a so-called upper bound, your opponent must use circumscribed polygons as well.

On the other hand, all you need to do is to sit there and take your time to explain the beauty of your approach to the king. What you did was indeed a *Monte Carlo simulation*. You can just wait for more and more data from your men until the end of the day.

Enough of role-playing for now, let's find out why 1000 men sprinkling 1000 grains repeatedly will give us a pretty good estimation of π.

Remember that π not only describes the relationship between the diameter and the perimeter but also the relationship of radius R and the area of a circle A. Here, C is the perimeter and D is the diameter:

$$C = \pi D$$

$$A = \pi R^2 = \frac{\pi}{4} D^2$$

Now, suppose one sand grain falls randomly on the square, what is the chance that this grain will be inside the circle? Well, it is kind of obvious: $\frac{A}{S}$ is the ratio of the circle's area and the square's area. It must also be the chance we are looking for as long as a good level of *randomness* is present.

Wait, we also have the expressions of A in terms of π, right? What will happen if we plug it in? Let me use P(*grain in circle*) to represent the chance that the grain will fall inside the circle. We have the following expressions:

$$
\begin{aligned}
P(grain\,in\,circle) &= \frac{circle's\,area}{square's\,area} \\
&= \frac{A}{S} \\
&= \frac{\frac{\pi}{4}D^2}{D^2} \\
&= \frac{\pi}{4}
\end{aligned}
$$

Surprise! The chance does *not* depend on the size of the square. The only issue is that such a beautiful claim is only theoretically true, we have to sample it to estimate such a probability. This is why you, the role-playing wise person, asked for tons of grains and 1000 careful men with sharp eyes to repeat these experiments. Each experiment will give you a value of π, and by the end of the day, we can take the average of all the experiment results.

The following is the Python code that does the simulation. Don't worry. I will explain it line by line. As you become more and more familiar with the style of this book, somewhat trivial stuff will be skipped in the future.

```python
import random
import numpy as np
random.seed(2021)
pi_values = list()
num_persons = 1000
num_rounds = 20
num_grains = 1000
edge = 10
for r in range(num_rounds):
    for p in range(num_persons):
        in_circle = 0
```

```
    for g in range(num_grains):
        x, y = (random.random() - 0.5)*edge, (random.random() -
        0.5)*edge
        if x**2 + y**2 <= (edge/2)**2:
            in_circle += 1
    pi = in_circle/num_grains * 4
    pi_values.append(pi)
print(np.mean(pi_values))
```

The code simulates 1000 men's grain sprinkling behavior, assuming each person can do 20 experiments a day. For each sprinkled grain, we calculate the coordinate of the grain using the `random.random()` function. Here, we assume the circle's center is at the origin.

To ensure the result is reproducible on your computer, I set the *random seed* to be 2021. Almost all randomness we see in computer science is called pseudorandomness. They are not completely random, just as the wise person's 1000 men would not truly uniformly sprinkle grains on the paper. However, for Python programming, in almost all cases, you can trust the high level of randomness of the built-in random number generator. Not all simulations in this book have a random seed though.

The `random.random()` function will return a random variable between *0* and *1*. See the visualization in Figure 1-3 to get a sense of how *1000* results of `random.random()` are distributed. It has a name: the *standard uniform distribution*.

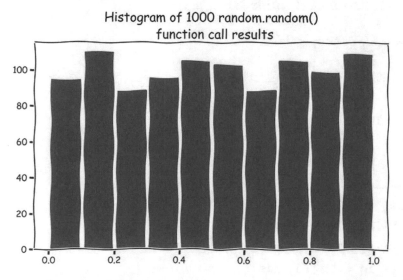

Figure 1-3. *Distribution of 1000 randomly generated numbers between 0 and 1*

The corresponding code that generates the visualization reads as follows:

```
random.seed(2021)
fig, ax = plt.subplots()
ax.hist([random.random() for _ in range(1000)], bins=10, rwidth=0.9)
ax.set_title("Histogram of 1000 random.random() results")
```

Next, let's visualize the one possible look among infinitely many possibilities of *1000* sprinkled grains in Figure 1-4.

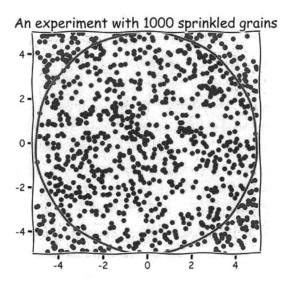

Figure 1-4. *1000 sprinkled grains in a square*

The code reads as follows:

```
random.seed(2021)
edge = 10
num_grains = 1000
with plt.xkcd():
    fig, ax = plt.subplots(figsize=(6, 6))
#    plt.axis("off")
    plt.axis("equal")
    ax.set_xlim(-edge/2, edge/2)
    ax.set_ylim(-edge/2, edge/2)
    xs_in, ys_in = list(), list()
    xs_out, ys_out = list(), list()
```

```python
for g in range(num_grains):
    x, y = (random.random() - 0.5)*edge, (random.random() - 0.5)*edge
    if x**2 + y**2 <= (edge/2)**2:
        xs_in.append(x)
        ys_in.append(y)
    else:
        xs_out.append(x)
        ys_out.append(y)
ax.scatter(xs_in, ys_in, color="r")
ax.scatter(xs_out, ys_out, color="b")
circle = plt.Circle((0, 0), edge/2, fill=False, color="g", lw=3)
ax.add_patch(circle)
ax.set_title("An experiment with 1000 sprinkled grains", fontsize=20)
```

I don't see any worrying concentration or bias in the visualization, do you? This means that a good level of *randomness* is present, so our approach of using area ratio to approach π is valid. Next, let's do a histogram plot of our 20K π values and see how spreading our results are. We obtain Figure 1-5.

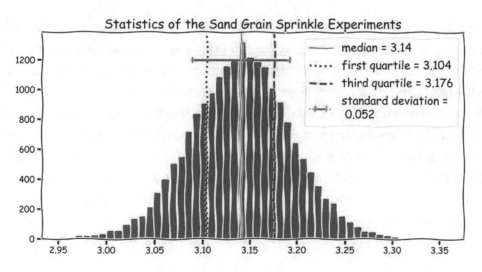

Figure 1-5. *Distribution of 20,000 calculated π values*

7

Note that the *mean* and *median* are so close to each other that only the median is plotted. There are three major points to obtain this visualization:

1. The *mean* and *median* are quite close to the ground truth value of π. This is a good sign because we know our data is not skewed by large outliers.

2. Quartiles are values that partition the data into equal-number segments. The first quartile being *3.104* indicates that 25% of the results are smaller than *3.104*. By the same idea, *25%* of the results are greater than *3.176*.

3. Standard deviation (*STD*), which is represented by the horizontal error bar, indicates the average deviation of a result from the sample mean. The standard deviation is about *0.052*.

The formula of a sample's standard deviation reads as follows:

$$STD = \sqrt{\frac{1}{N-1}\sum_{i=1}^{N}\left(x_i - \overline{x}\right)^2}$$

Here, $\overline{x}$ represents the mean of the sample, and N is the total number of samples. The standard deviation quantifies how confident we are about our result. In general, the smaller the standard deviation is, the more concentrated our results are around the mean; therefore, we are more confident about our results.

You may also notice the beautiful curve of the histogram. There is a reason behind that. Here is a brief teaser. The distribution of simulated π values follows a so-called normal distribution. It is a consequence of the famous *central limit theorem* (CLT). The key idea is that under a bunch of quite loose conditions, quantities we observe in nature tend to follow a bell-curve distribution. Such quantities include our weights of a rather large population, length of tree leaves in a forest, etc.

The code snippet that generates the preceding visualizations reads as follows:

```
with plt.xkcd():
    fig, ax = plt.subplots(figsize=(12, 6))
    ax.hist(pi_values, bins=50, rwidth=0.8)
    pi_mean = np.mean(pi_values)
    pi_median = np.median(pi_values)
    # pi_mean and pi_median are very close. Only median is plotted.
```

```python
pi_std = np.std(pi_values)
pi_quartiles = np.quantile(pi_values, [0, 0.25, 0.5, 0.75, 1])
ax.set_title(
    "Statistics of the Sand Grain Sprinkle Experiments", fontsize=20)
line_1 = ax.axvline(pi_mean, color='red', lw=1)
line_2 = ax.axvline(pi_quartiles[1],
                    color='purple',
                    lw=3,
                    linestyle="dotted")
line_3 = ax.axvline(pi_quartiles[3],
                    color='green',
                    lw=3,
                    linestyle="dashed")
std_bar = ax.errorbar(pi_mean, 1200,
                      xerr=pi_std,
                      capsize=5,
                      elinewidth=3,
                      markeredgewidth=2,
                      linestyle=":")
ax.legend([line_1, line_2, line_3, std_bar],
          ["median = {}".format(pi_median),
           "first quartile = {}".format(pi_quartiles[1]),
           "third quartile = {}".format(pi_quartiles[3]),
           "standard deviation =\n {}".format(round(pi_std, 3))],
          fontsize=18)
```

Going back to the role-playing, before your opponent could produce a four-significant-digit number, say *3.1416*, he would find that his pen was too thick for him to further section the circle. You, on the other hand, could show the early results to the king. As your men keep reporting new results, the confidence you have in the result will increase.

Before moving on to the next subsection where Monte Carlo simulation *precedes* the exact analytical solution for more than 200 years, I prepared some exercises for you to enhance your understanding of Monte Carlo simulation. You may need to utilize the *numpy* library's vectorized computation to accelerate the computation.

Exercise

1. Verify that this is true that the simulation doesn't depend on the length of the edges.

2. Suppose the king is obsessed with your simulation. Now you have one million people at your command for the calculation. Utilize *numpy*'s vectorized computation to perform the simulation. Perform the statistics calculation as well. Did you find the relationship between the number of results and the standard deviation? Can you plot the relationship between the two values?

3. Can you compute the volume of a five-dimensional unit ball using Monte Carlo simulation? Note that this question is deliberately vague. Do some research and enjoy the exploration.

Contain the Goat!

I hope you enjoy the Middle East adventure in the 16th century. Now, let's time travel to Great Britain in the 1800s. You had a problem at hand to solve as a shepherd.

You own a land with a bizarre circular shape. Well, it has to be circular; otherwise, there is no fun! You also had a very naughty goat who had to be on leash. Otherwise, the goat would eat everything in its reach and had congestion issues.

Now, you had to stick one end of the leash to one point of the circular fence; how long should the leash be so the goat can exactly reach half of your land? Figure 1-6 is a visualization of the problem. Here, for simplicity, we can set the radius of your land to be *1*.

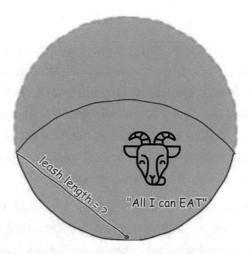

Figure 1-6. *A leashed goat is contained inside round fences*

This problem is the so-called interior grazing problem. It has been known for 200 years, but the analytical solution was only found in early 2020.

$$\gamma = 2\cos\left(\frac{1}{2}\frac{\oint_{|z-3\pi/8|=\pi/4} z/(\sin z - z\cos z - \pi/2)dz}{\oint_{|z-3\pi/8|=\pi/4} 1/(\sin z - z\cos z - \pi/2)dz}\right).$$

However, with the Monte Carlo simulation we just discussed, you can calculate the length of the leash by writing several lines of Python code.

The naive idea is the same as the sand grain sprinkling one. First, you generate a uniformly distributed random point inside your land, then you check whether the goat can reach that point or not given a leash length. After enough sampling, if the goat can reach more than half of the area, shorten the leash; otherwise, increase it. We can repeat this process until the desired precision is achieved.

You may notice that the preceding method is not computationally optimal. A better way is to generate enough points first, then determine the length of the leash later. We will approach the computation in this improved way later.

What Randomness?

Wait a minute, we have an ambiguity here. It is easy to imagine a uniformly distributed random point inside a *square*: you just make it uniform on one side and uniform on another side as well. However, what does it mean to have a uniformly distributed random point inside a *circle*? How would you generate tens of thousands of such points?

You have two options:

1. You only care about a circle, but you use a square that exactly circumscribes the circle to do the work. You still generate uniformly distributed points in the square but discard those that fall outside of the circle. You use these that fall inside the circle to do the calculation. This does guarantee the same kind of uniformity, but the roaring CPU will probably not be happy because only about *78.5%* of its work is honored.

2. Another option is to use the polar coordinate as shown in Figure 1-7. First, you generate a uniformly distributed radius between *0* and the radius of your land, say, *R*, then you generate a uniformly distributed radian value between *0* degree and *360* degrees. The location of the point is also uniquely determined.

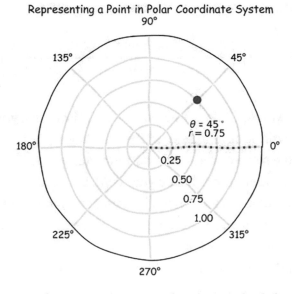

Figure 1-7. *A polar coordinate system can also uniquely define a point on a 2-D plane*

In the example illustrated earlier, a point in 2-D space is uniquely determined by a pair (θ, γ) where θ is the angle that the point rotates counter-clockwise against the $\theta = 0$ line, which is represented by the dotted line. γ is the distance between the dot and the origin. θ takes values between 0° and 360°, while γ can be any positive number.

The transformation between normal Cartesian coordinates and polar coordinates can be obtained using the following formula:

$$x = \gamma \cos\theta$$
$$y = \gamma \sin\theta$$
$$\gamma^2 = x^2 + y^2$$

The following is the code snippet for the polar coordinate system demonstration. It will give you a good sense of how to manipulate objects with polar coordinates:

```python
from matplotlib.patches import Arc
with plt.xkcd():
    fig, ax_polar = plt.subplots(figsize=(6, 6),
                                 subplot_kw={'projection': 'polar'})
    ax_polar.set_rmax(1)
    ax_polar.set_rticks([0.25, 0.5, 0.75, 1],)
    ax_polar.set_rlabel_position(-60)
    ax_polar.grid(True, linewidth=3, alpha=0.4)
    ax_polar.set_axisbelow(True)
    ax_polar.plot([0, 0], [0, 1.2], lw=3, color="red",
                  linestyle="dotted")
    ax_polar.scatter([np.pi/4], [0.75], s=120, color="blue")
    ax_polar.text(np.pi/7, 0.5, r"$\theta$ = $45^\circ$")
    ax_polar.text(np.pi/12, 0.45, r"$r = 0.75$")
    ax_polar.set_title("Representing a Point in Polar Coordinate System",
                       fontsize=20)
```

Now, which option would you choose? They both sound valid, aren't they? Let the numbers speak for themselves. The following code snippets generate 10,000 random points in a circle with both approaches. Let's find out by visualizing the distribution of the generated points.

Setting the length of the leash to *1.25*, option 1 gives us Figure 1-8.

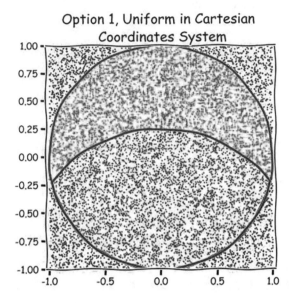

Figure 1-8. *Results from sampling with the Cartesian coordinate*

The statistics in Table 1-1 tell us how many points will not be used because they fall out of the circle and how many are reachable by the goat, etc.

Table 1-1. *Number of grains in each region for Cartesian coordinate system sampling*

Outside Points	Unreachable Points	Reachable Points
2101	3443	4456

If option 1 is correct, this actually means that *1.25* is probably too long. And roughly *20%* of our CPU time is *wasted*.

Let's look at the result produced by option 2 as shown in Figure 1-9.

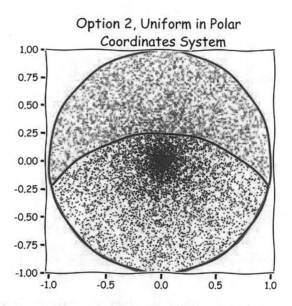

Figure 1-9. *Results from sampling with the polar coordinate*

If option 2 is correct, we have no wasted CPU time, but the statistics look concerning. I counted the numbers in Table 1-2.

Table 1-2. *Number of grains in each region for polar coordinate system sampling*

Outside Points	Unreachable Points	Reachable Points
0	3230	6770

The source codes for the plotting are too long and therefore omitted. However, they should be straightforward to reproduce.

Alrighty, take a look at the scatter plot of these points; which one looks more random? It is kind of obvious that option 1 demonstrates a higher level of randomness than option 2. This becomes more clear if we zoom in to option 2's result as shown in Figure 1-10.

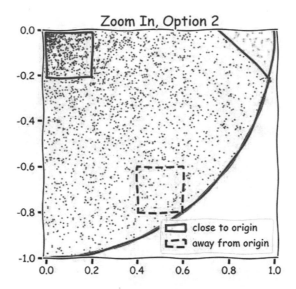

Figure 1-10. *Density imbalance becomes clear if we zoom in to the polar coordinate system's result*

The two square areas obviously contain different numbers of points. The one closer to the origin contains more points, and the one further away from the origin contains fewer.

The reason is that a uniform distribution will be distorted if you *transform* the coordinate system. Although the points are uniformly distributed in terms of the polar coordinates, the transformation using trigonometry formulas distorts them so they are no longer uniformly distributed in the Cartesian coordinates. This definitely rings an alarming bell.

The following code snippet will estimate the length of the leash using the bisection method. Of course, you can change the position of the other end of the leash, but we will stick with the simple one at the lower bottom of the land. Note we are going to use the result from option 1 since it is the correct simulation.

The bisection method is a root-finding method. Here, we simply borrow the idea. Because the number of reachable points monotonically grows as the length of the leash increases. Let's say we start finding the length in range [0, 2], and we start with the middle point *1*; if more than half of the points are reachable, we begin searching in [0, 1] and start with the new middle point *0.5*. By the same token, if there are fewer than half of the points reachable, we pick *1.5* as the new middle and search in range [1, 2]. The iteration continues until a stop condition satisfies.

```python
random.seed(2021)
num_points = 10000
num_valid_points = 0
xs, ys = list(), list()
for g in range(num_points):
    x, y = (random.random() - 0.5)*2, (random.random() - 0.5)*2
    if x**2 + y**2 <= 1:
        xs.append(x)
        ys.append(y)
        num_valid_points += 1

# begin bisection
low, high, middle = 0, 2, 1
epsilon = 0.001
while high-low > epsilon:
    reachable = sum((x-0)**2 + (y - (-1))**2 <= (middle)
                    ** 2 for x, y in zip(xs, ys))
    if reachable > num_valid_points//2:  # need to shorten the leash
        low, high, middle = low, middle, (low+middle)/2
    elif reachable < num_valid_points//2:  # need to increase the leash
        low, high, middle = middle, high, (middle+high)/2
    else:
        break

print(middle)  # 1.15869140625
```

Alright, I bet you feel the essence of Monte Carlo simulation. In both the calculation of π and the containment of the goat, we are facing deterministic problems that involve no randomness at all. However, by introducing randomness, we turn analytical problems into simulation problems. This is the power of Monte Carlo simulation. In the next section, we are going to explore another kind of problem which involves randomness intrinsically.

Now, finish the following exercise before jumping onto the second stage of the rocket.

Exercise

1. Suppose the goat is in a space station, find the solution in three dimensions such that the goat can only reach half of the volume of a unit ball.

2. Improve the performance of the bisection algorithm by only considering fewer critical points around the boundaries.

3. Let's say we are not satisfied with a single fixed point on the fence. Can you pick other points on the fence to perform the calculation of leash length? Do you get similar results? What does the distribution of your results look like?

Summary

In this chapter, we studied the classic use case of Monte Carlo simulation: the calculation of π. We researched the effects of *randomness* on the validity of the calculation and investigated the distribution of our simulation results.

CHAPTER 2

Markov Chain, a Peek into the Future

In this chapter, we continue our exploration in the world of simulation. Different from the previous Monte Carlo simulation where the scenario is purely static, which means there is no dynamics in the simulation, we are going to study dynamics of a system.

The Markov chain, specifically the discrete-time Markov chain, is named after Russian mathematician Andrey Andreyevich Markov. He is a pioneer in the study of stochastic processes and the first to introduce the concept of Markov chains.

Let's introduce the Markov chain with a simple example of weather forecasting.

Weather Forecasting

Suppose we have a weather forecasting system that predicts the weather in the next hour. The weather can only take three possibilities: sunny, cloudy, or rainy. Here, we call these possibilities the *states*. We won't predict the weather continuously but rather forecast the weather in the next hour. This makes our system *discrete*.

The continuous-time Markov chain is beyond the scope of this book. It requires more rigorous analysis. However, the fundamental ideas of the discrete-time Markov chain remain unchanged.

Weather will change so there is a probability that a sunny day will turn into a cloudy day. Similarly, a cloudy day will turn into a rainy day, etc. We can define the transition probabilities in Table 2-1. The columns represent the current weather states, and the rows represent the next hour's.

R. Li and A. Nakano, *Simulation with Python*, https://doi.org/10.1007/978-1-4842-8185-7_2

Table 2-1. *Weather transition probabilities*

	Sunny	**Cloudy**	**Rainy**
Sunny (next hour)	$\dfrac{1}{2}$	$\dfrac{1}{3}$	$\dfrac{2}{3}$
Cloudy (next hour)	$\dfrac{1}{3}$	$\dfrac{1}{3}$	$\dfrac{1}{6}$
Rainy (next hour)	$\dfrac{1}{6}$	$\dfrac{1}{3}$	$\dfrac{1}{6}$

The way to interpret the table is to read it column-wise. For example, if the current weather is sunny, then the probability of the next hour's weather being cloudy is $\dfrac{1}{3}$. This is indicated by the second row in the first column (besides the row name column).

We can also denote this probability by the *transition probability* notation. Let's use s_i to denote the state of the weather at hour i. Then the previous transition probability can be denoted as follows:

$$P_{sunny->cloudy} = P\big(s_1 = cloudy \big| s_0 = sunny\big) = \frac{1}{3}$$

We used the notation of conditional probability in the expression $P(s_1 = cloudy | s_0 = sunny)$. It simply means that given the weather at the previous hour is sunny, which is a *condition*, the probability of the weather at the next hour being cloudy is $\dfrac{1}{3}$.

With the definition of transition probability, we can use a graph to represent the weather forecast. The graph shown in Figure 2-1 illustrates this.

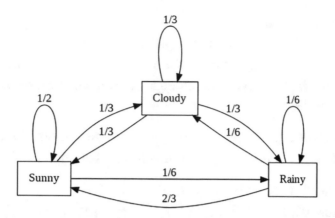

Figure 2-1. *A graph representing the weather forecast based upon transition probability*

Well, what does this even mean? How can we use the table or the graph to forecast weather? The idea is quite simple; we start from a current weather, a.k.a. a state, then transition to other possible states according to the transition probabilities. For example, if the current state is sunny, then at the next hour, we have a chance of $\frac{1}{2}$ to remain sunny, a chance of $\frac{1}{3}$ to become cloudy, etc. This looks easy so far. How about the next weather? We have to combine all possible *trajectories* to do the forecast. For example, the sunny state can be achieved from three different trajectories, from being sunny, being cloudy, and being rainy, which gives us the following combined probability:

$$P\left(s_2 = sunny\right) = \frac{1}{2}\frac{1}{2} + \frac{1}{3}\frac{1}{3} + \frac{1}{6}\frac{2}{3} = \frac{17}{36}$$

It is still *possible* to continue the calculation manually, but we would like to leave the labor to computers.

Formally speaking, a system like we just introduced must satisfy two important properties to be a Markov chain:

1.   The first one is called the *Markovian* or *memoryless* property. It means that the system will only remember the immediate past state but not further. For example, the weather forecast system will only remember and use the current weather to forecast the next hour's weather but not previous hours' weathers.

2. The second one should be treated as a simplification, which can be removed if you want to match real-world scenarios. It is that our Markov transition probabilities are fixed regardless of the time index *i*. In real life, as seasons change, our transition probabilities should change.

The following is the code snippet to automate the calculation. Notice that I already used the matrix notation to represent the transition probability:

```
sunny_to = {"sunny":1/2, "cloudy":1/3,"rainy":1/6}
cloudy_to = {"sunny":1/3, "cloudy":1/3,"rainy":1/3}
rainy_to = {"sunny":2/3, "cloudy":1/6,"rainy":1/6}

state = {"sunny":1, "cloudy":0,"rainy":0}
weathers = ["sunny","cloudy","rainy"]
for _ in range(10):
    next_state = {}
    for weather in weathers:
        next_state[weather] = (sunny_to[weather] * state["sunny"] +
                               cloudy_to[weather] * state["cloudy"] +
                               rainy_to[weather] * state["rainy"])
    state = next_state
    print(state)
```

The result looks like the following. You can check that the probabilities roughly sum up to unit 1:

```
{'sunny': 0.5, 'cloudy': 0.3333333333333333, 'rainy': 0.16666666666666666}
{'sunny': 0.4722222222222222, 'cloudy': 0.3055555555555556, 'rainy':
0.2222222222222222}
{'sunny': 0.4861111111111111, 'cloudy': 0.2962962962962963, 'rainy':
0.2175925925925926}
{'sunny': 0.4868827160493827, 'cloudy': 0.2970679012345679, 'rainy':
0.21604938271604937}
{'sunny': 0.48649691358024694, 'cloudy': 0.2973251028806584, 'rainy':
0.21617798353909465}
{'sunny': 0.48647548010973934, 'cloudy': 0.29730366941015085, 'rainy':
0.21622085048010972}
```

{'sunny': 0.4864861968449931, 'cloudy': 0.29729652491998165, 'rainy': 0.21621727823502512}
{'sunny': 0.4864867922191738, 'cloudy': 0.29729712029416244, 'rainy': 0.21621608748666357}
{'sunny': 0.4864864945320834, 'cloudy': 0.29729731875222265, 'rainy': 0.2162161867156937}
{'sunny': 0.48648647799391176, 'cloudy': 0.29729730221405093, 'rainy': 0.21621621979203703}

In the nested for loop, we implemented the logic that one state can be achieved through multiple paths. For example, the weather after 3 hours can be essentially achieved through $3^3 = 27$ different paths.

The preceding code can be written in a much more concise way using matrix notation as follows. If you do the math, you will see that the matrix multiplication operation matches the system evolution operation exactly. To run the following code, you need to install the *numpy* library as *np* per the Python community convention:

```
tm = np.array([[1/2,1/3,2/3],
               [1/3,1/3,1/6],
               [1/6,1/3,1/6]])
state = np.array([1,0,0])
for _ in range(10):
    state = tm@state
    print(state)
```

Now, let's visualize the probabilities of each weather as illustrated in Figure 2-2.

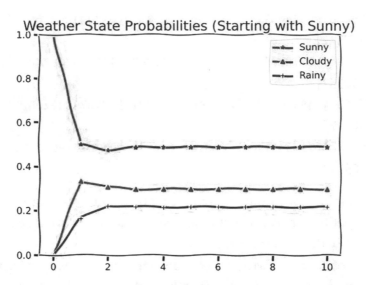

Figure 2-2. *Weather state probabilities for ten iterations, starting with sunny weather*

What's going on here? Why are the probabilities stale after, say, the third iteration? Before moving on to the explanation, let's take a look at another initial condition. How about starting with rainy weather? You can check the simulation result in Figure 2-3.

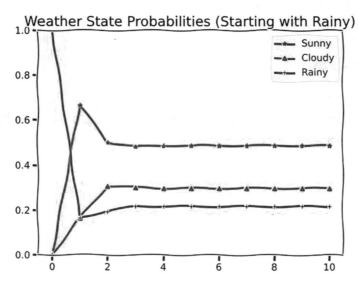

Figure 2-3. *Weather state probabilities for ten iterations, starting with rainy weather*

Indeed, it looks like not only we reach a stable distribution, the distribution is also independent of our initial weather.

Eigenstates of Markov Chains

Is there anything special about the stable probability distribution $\vec{x} \approx [0.486, 0.297, 0.216]$? It turns out that it is an eigenvector of the transition matrix with an eigenvalue of 1. In other words, it represents the *eigenstate* of the Markov chain. One can actually decompose any square matrix to find out its eigenvalues and eigenvectors. You can use `numpy.linalg.eig(tm)[0]` to obtain the eigenvalues of the matrix *tm* and use `numpy.linalg.eig(tm)[1]` to obtain the corresponding eigenvectors.

Note that eigenstate has a special meaning in quantum mechanics. Here, I just borrow the word as it makes sense in this context. It also has other names like stationary distribution, equilibrium distribution, limit distribution, etc.

First, let's take a look at the transition matrix as already being used in the previous simulation. We use $\vec{x'}$ and $\vec{x}$ to denote the new (next hour) and old (current hour) states, respectively. The transition matrix is denoted by T:

$$\vec{x'} = T\vec{x}$$
(1)

$$= \begin{bmatrix} \dfrac{1}{2} & \dfrac{1}{3} & \dfrac{2}{3} \\ \dfrac{1}{3} & \dfrac{1}{3} & \dfrac{1}{6} \\ \dfrac{1}{6} & \dfrac{1}{3} & \dfrac{2}{6} \end{bmatrix} \begin{pmatrix} 0.48648649 \\ 0.2972973 \\ 0.21621622 \end{pmatrix}$$
(2)

$$\approx \begin{pmatrix} 0.48648649 \\ 0.2972973 \\ 0.21621622 \end{pmatrix}$$
(3)

$$= \vec{x}$$
(4)

Note that the calculation ignores some negligible precision-caused numerical errors.

This equation tells us once our system reaches the eigenstate, it will remain there for the rest of the transition. This means that after several hours, the probability of being sunny will be about 50% regardless of the current weather. The matrix notation also enlightens us that the evolution of the system can also be written as the multiplication of a series of matrices. For simplicity, I reuse the notation of s_n. You have already seen s_i, right? They are basically the same thing.

$$s_n = T s_{n-1} \tag{1}$$

$$= T^2 s_{n-2} \tag{2}$$

$$= T^n s_0 \tag{3}$$

$$\approx \begin{bmatrix} 0.49 & 0.49 & 0.49 \\ 0.30 & 0.30 & 0.30 \\ 0.22 & 0.22 & 0.22 \end{bmatrix} s_0 \tag{4}$$

As you can see, no matter our initial state s_0 is, as long as the elements sum up to 1, the output, s_n is the eigenstate. This is a remarkable fact.

You may ask whether all transition matrices give such a nice property. The answer is no. Here is an example:

```
tm = np.array([[0, 0, 1],
               [1, 0, 0],
               [0, 1, 0]])
state = np.array([1,0,0])
for _ in range(10):
    state = tm@state
    print(state)
```

Without running this code, can you guess what the states look like? Our transition matrix basically says that a sunny day will *definitely* become a cloudy day and a cloudy day will become a rainy day, etc. You may expect the following output:

```
[0 1 0]
[0 0 1]
[1 0 0]
[0 1 0]
...
```

Another issue is the rate of convergence. The preceding example shows that sometimes the probabilities may never converge. Here is another transition matrix that converges slower than the earlier one we discussed. Feel free to try it on your own.

$$\begin{bmatrix} 0.00 & 0.05 & 0.98 \\ 0.99 & 0.00 & 0.02 \\ 0.01 & 0.95 & 0.00 \end{bmatrix}$$

Exercise

1. Find out the eigenstates of the transition matrix with a slower convergence rate.

2. All of our previous simulation is based on analytical probability calculation. Can you do a simulation that just picks a random weather and evolves it according to the transition probabilities? Let's say you do it for 10,000 steps, which is roughly 400 days, and count how many of these 10,000 data points are sunny, cloudy, and rainy. What's your expectation? Does your discovery agree with your expectation?

Markov Chain Applications

In this section, let's look at two interesting applications of the Markov chain. First, let's look at how the Markov chain can be used to answer a nontrivial probability question. Then, we will use the Markov chain as a generative model to generate some natural languages.

A Random Walk That Has an End

Suppose you have a fruit-loving tortoise that moves in a tube. The tube is 7 inches long. At the left end, there is a banana, and at the right end, there is an apple. Now, the tortoise starts at a position that is 3 inches away from the left end, which means it is closer to the banana than the apple by 1 inch. The tortoise can only move 1 inch per minute, and it moves randomly to the left or to the right with equal probability. The tortoise is so active that it *will* move every minute until it reaches one of the fruits. The setting can be visualized as in Figure 2-4.

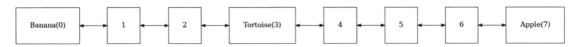

Figure 2-4. *A graph that represents the states the tortoise can be in*

The question is, what are the probabilities that the tortoise *eventually* reaches the banana and apple?

Spend some time to think about the question yourself. Here are some intuitions and observations:

1. Given enough time, intuitively the tortoise will reach one of the fruits. Our tube is just 7 inches long, and the tortoise just keeps moving.

2. The tortoise should have a higher, probably not much, probability of reaching the banana than the apple. The setting is not symmetric.

Let's perform a set of simulation runs to directly simulate such a system and evaluate such probabilities:

```
def tortoise_run(state = 3, left_prob = 0.5):
    steps = 0
    while state % 7 != 0:
        if np.random.random() < left_prob:
            state -= 1
        else:
            state += 1
        steps += 1
```

```
if state == 0:
    return steps, 0
else:
    return steps, 7
```

We can run the simulation for 10,000 times and count how many times the tortoise reaches the banana and apple. I can plot the result with the following code:

```
simulations = [tortoise_run()  for _ in range(10000)]

bananas = np.array([x[1] == 0 for x in simulations]).cumsum()
apples = np.array([x[1] == 7 for x in simulations]).cumsum()

with plt.xkcd():
    fig, ax = plt.subplots(figsize=(8,6))
    plt.plot(bananas/(bananas+apples), lw=3,label="bananas")
    plt.plot(apples/(bananas+apples), lw=3,label="apples")
    plt.legend()
    plt.title("Probabilities of Reaching Bananas/Apples")
    plt.xlabel("# of runs")
```

The result looks like Figure 2-5.

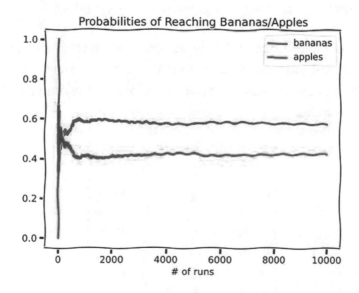

Figure 2-5. *Probabilities that the tortoise reaches bananas or apples for 10,000 runs*

It does agree with our intuition that the tortoise is slightly more likely to reach the banana. If you check the end of the bananas/(bananas+apples) array, you will find that the probability of reaching the banana is about *0.575*.

As an in-chapter exercise, you can plot a histogram to check the distribution of the number of steps before the tortoise stops moving. I am going to leave this as an exercise. Your result should look like the one in Figure 2-6. Note that the x axis is in log scale.

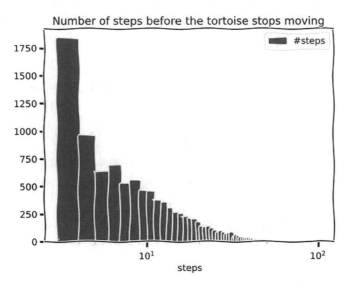

Figure 2-6. *Number of steps before the tortoise stops moving*

Now, let's use our knowledge of the Markov chain to find the exact probabilities in the original question. If you think about it, the tortoise's random walk can be treated as a Markov chain that has the following transition matrix. The dimension matches the number of possible states.

$$
\begin{bmatrix}
1 & \frac{1}{2} & 0 & 0 & 0 & 0 & 0 & 0 \\
0 & 0 & \frac{1}{2} & 0 & 0 & 0 & 0 & 0 \\
0 & \frac{1}{2} & 0 & \frac{1}{2} & 0 & 0 & 0 & 0 \\
0 & 0 & \frac{1}{2} & 0 & \frac{1}{2} & 0 & 0 & 0 \\
0 & 0 & 0 & \frac{1}{2} & 0 & \frac{1}{2} & 0 & 0 \\
0 & 0 & 0 & 0 & \frac{1}{2} & 0 & \frac{1}{2} & 0 \\
0 & 0 & 0 & 0 & 0 & \frac{1}{2} & 0 & 0 \\
0 & 0 & 0 & 0 & 0 & 0 & \frac{1}{2} & 1
\end{bmatrix}
$$

This Markov chain is different from the weather one mainly because it has two so-called *absorbing states*. The absorbing states are the left and right ends of the tube. Once the tortoise reaches one of the ends, it stops moving. The first and the last element in the transition matrix diagonal are *1* which indicate the absorbing states.

Now, let's find out the *eigenstate* of the multiple-step transition matrix. The idea is that we treat multiple continuous transitions, say, 50 steps, as one transition and consider its transition matrix. You can find the transition matrix for *50* steps using the one-liner `reduce(lambda x,y:x@y,[tortoise_tm for _ in range(50)])`. If you change *50* to a larger number, the matrix remains largely the same up to a precision error.

$$
\begin{bmatrix}
1.00 & 0.86 & 0.71 & 0.57 & 0.43 & 0.28 & 0.14 & 0.00 \\
0.00 & 0.00 & 0.00 & 0.00 & 0.00 & 0.00 & 0.00 & 0.00 \\
0.00 & 0.00 & 0.00 & 0.00 & 0.00 & 0.00 & 0.00 & 0.00 \\
0.00 & 0.00 & 0.00 & 0.00 & 0.00 & 0.00 & 0.00 & 0.00 \\
0.00 & 0.00 & 0.00 & 0.00 & 0.00 & 0.00 & 0.00 & 0.00 \\
0.00 & 0.00 & 0.00 & 0.00 & 0.00 & 0.00 & 0.00 & 0.00 \\
0.00 & 0.00 & 0.00 & 0.00 & 0.00 & 0.00 & 0.00 & 0.00 \\
0.00 & 0.14 & 0.28 & 0.43 & 0.57 & 0.71 & 0.86 & 1.00
\end{bmatrix}
$$

The symmetry is pretty clear. The closer the tortoise is to the left end, the more likely it will be to reach the banana. The highest probability is *0.86*. This agrees with our intuition as the tortoise does have a chance to reach for the apple although the banana is just 1 inch away. We multiply the transition matrix with the initial state `numpy.array([0,0,0,1,0,0,0,0])` to get the probability of reaching the banana eventually. Note that it does agree with our simulation performed earlier.

Alright. This is the end of our first section. You have seen how to use the Markov chain to predict the weather and simulate a hungry tortoise movement. Next, let's try to use the Markov chain as a generative model to write some poems.

Sonnet Written by Drunk Shakespeare

A Markov chain can be used to model human language as a simplistic first approach. Human language has intrinsic patterns such that the probabilities that a certain word follows another word are very different. A Markov chain fits in this scenario perfectly.

Let's try to grab some sonnets from Shakespeare and turn his text into a Markov chain with corresponding probabilities.

First, we need to process the raw text by removing the punctuation, etc. We are going to use a third-party library called "nltk" to do the lemmatization. However, we will build the Markov chain on our own. If you are interested in comparing your result with output from mature libraries, check this repository. The text file that contains the sonnets is the *sonnet.txt* file, which is provided in the associated GitHub repo. You can also find the sonnets on the Project Gutenberg website.

Lemmatization is a process of converting a word or phrase into its base form. For example, the word "dogs" is converted to "dog," and the word "went" is converted to "go." This is helpful because our sonnet dataset is not that large that reducing words with different forms, but similar meaning, to the same one can centralize our transition probabilities somehow. You are free to explore the nonlemmatized version and compare the differences.

Here is a sample from the text file:

> *From fairest creatures we desire increase,*
> *That thereby beauty's rose might never die,*
> *But as the riper should by time decease,*
> *His tender heir might bear his memory:*
> *But thou contracted to thine own bright eyes,*
> *Feed'st thy light's flame with self-substantial fuel,*
> *Making a famine where abundance lies,*
> *Thy self thy foe, to thy sweet self too cruel:*
> *Thou that art now the world's fresh ornament,*
> *And only herald to the gaudy spring,*
> *Within thine own bud buriest thy content,*
> *And, tender churl, mak'st waste in niggarding:*
> *Pity the world, or else this glutton be,*
> *To eat the world's due, by the grave and thee.*

The sonnets are separated with empty lines. The following code will preprocess each sentence, which can be incomplete, to lowercases and punctuation-free:

```
# sonnet preprocessing
import string
import nltk
from nltk.stem.wordnet import WordNetLemmatizer
# nltk.download('wordnet')
lemmatizer = WordNetLemmatizer()
```

```
sonnet_path = "../../code_examples/chap2/sonnet.txt"
with open(sonnet_path,"r") as fp:
    sonnets = fp.readlines()

sonnets = [sentence.strip().lower().replace("'s","") for sentence in
sonnets if sentence != "\n" ]
sonnets = ["".join([char for char in sentence if char not in string.
punctuation]) for sentence in sonnets]
```

Note that you may need to uncomment the *wordnet* download line to download additional data. The sonnets variable is a list of sentences. We are simplifying the problem by only handling lowercases and ignoring the punctuation like *beauty's*, which becomes *beauty*.

Now, let's build a defaultdict to store the counting from each word to its next word existing in the sonnets. Such word pairs are also called *bigrams*.

```
from collections import defaultdict
transition_dict = defaultdict(lambda : defaultdict(int))

for sentence in sonnets:
    words = list(filter(lambda x: len(x.strip()) > 0, sentence.split(" ")))
    words_pairs = [(lemmatizer.lemmatize(words[i]),lemmatizer.
    lemmatize(words[i+1])) for i in range(len(words)-1)]
    for (word_from, word_to) in words_pairs:
        transition_dict[word_from][word_to] += 1
```

Before using the *transition_dict* to generate sentences, let's take a look at the paths for the bigrams. The following visualization simply uses the width of edges to represent the frequency of the bigram. As it is not possible to show all edges, we use the *count_threshold* variable to control the number of transitional edges a word can have to connect to the next word:

```
# sonnet
from graphviz import Digraph

count_threshold = 10

# dot, fdp, neato, circo, twopi, and osage.

G = Digraph('G',format='png',engine='neato')
font_size = "300"
```

```python
G.attr('graph', pad='1', ranksep='1', nodesep='1')
G.attr('node', shape='circle', fixedsize='true')
G.attr(overlap="false")

for word_from in transition_dict.keys():
    for word_to in transition_dict[word_from].keys():
        lw = transition_dict[word_from][word_to]
        if lw > count_threshold:
            G.edge(word_from, word_to, penwidth=str(lw*0.1),label=str(lw))

G.view("sonnet")
```

The result looks like a big spider web as in Figure 2-7.

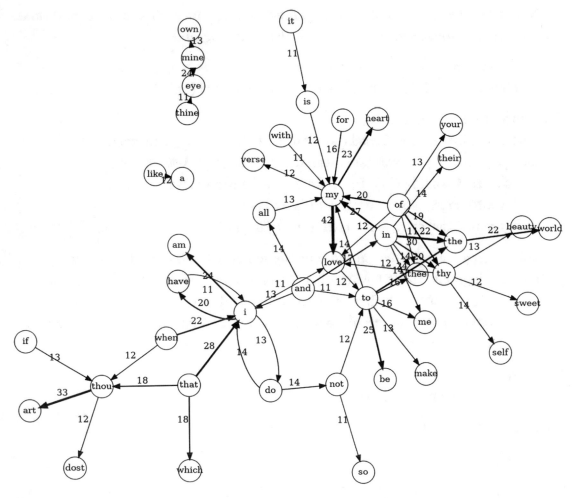

Figure 2-7. *The transitional relationship between words*

You can try to manipulate the value of the edge threshold. You will be able to see more fine structures at the cost of more overlapping edges.

Now, we can use the *transition_dict* to generate a sentence. Here is an example that I start with *i* and keep adding words to the sentence until there is no matching in the *transition_dict*:

```python
def sample_according_to_value(to_dict:dict):
    # return a key that corresponds to the value as frequency
    keys, freqs = [],[]
    for key,val in to_dict.items():
        keys.append(key)
        freqs.append(val)
    freqs = np.array(freqs)
    freqs = freqs/sum(freqs)
    return np.random.choice(keys,p=freqs)

def generate_sentence(start_word = "i", transition_dict = transition_dict,
hard_limit = 14):
    word = start_word
    sentence = []
    while word in transition_dict and len(sentence) < hard_limit:
        sentence.append(word)
        word = sample_according_to_value(transition_dict[word])
    sentence.append(word)
    return " ".join(sentence)

generate_sentence()
```

I got the following:

i praise that keep thee lie onward and lovely argument too much a foe commend.

I set a hard limit of *14* words in a sentence and generated a sonnet. The modification is trivial so I leave it to you. Here is what I got:

doom and the rest forgot upon my mistress over wrack
always write of their rank before the dead wood whose worth in it in them
wear this book of forebemoaned moan the rose have given thee i my
heart right
hindmost hold his memory death eternal slave to register and wrinkle
graven there reign love
authorizing thy part wa false painting set a far remote where your sound-
less deep a
audit canst thou not be it not for my lameness and by that million of
brain inhearse
epitaph to whom thou take them say thy picture sight would have any
be brought
leapt with the gentle thou hast thou dost advance
tonguetied muse brings forth your broad main doth nightly make the bla-
zon of that heaven
added feather to lay upon thy beauty wear this purpose laid by this
shall burn
tempest and no matter then did i may be taken
shower are mine eye corrupt by thy lusty day they themselves a the
world common
wrong than hawk and beauty thou be scorned like her wish i see what merit

Not bad, isn't it? Just look at this sentence: *tempest and no matter then did i may be taken*. It reads like something Shakespeare would write when he was drunk.

Alrighty. This concludes this chapter. Before moving on to our next chapter, here are some exercises.

Exercise

1. Can you adjust the transition probability matrix of the tortoise's movement to make it more realistic? For example, the tortoise can perhaps smell the fruit's scent when it's near and move toward it. How will the change impact the result?

2. For the tortoise problem, if you try to find the eigenvalues of the transition matrix, you should see two identical eigenvalues and some others. What are the repeated eigenvalues? What is the implication of the repeated eigenvalues?

3. Can you try *trigram* instead of *bigram* in the text generation?

4. Try to use a large corpus to improve the accuracy of your text generation model. For example, *nltk* has a large corpus of English texts. You can download the corpus from here.

Summary

We continue our journey of simulating using randomness. We studied the Markov chain model and learned the mathematics behind it. We applied the Markovian model to weather prediction, absorbing state cases, and the sonnet writing.

CHAPTER 3

Multi-armed Bandits, Probability Simulation, and Bayesian Statistics

Bob walks into a casino at dusk. He wants to try his luck as much as possible tonight. He begins playing the slot machine game which is simple and straightforward: you get three same symbols, you win. There are three different machines in the lobby, and Bob has 100 dollars to spend.

Bob knows that these machines have different probabilities of winning, and each pull will cost him 1 dollar. The question now is to find the best winning strategy for Bob.

A slot machine is also called a one-armed bandit. This question is also known as the classical *multi-armed bandit* problem.

Let's think of the edge cases first. If we have a lot of money, we can spend a good amount of money on each machine to obtain a good estimate of the winning probability, right? No investment, no gain. If we have little money, we can't afford to spend a lot of money on each machine, so we can only rely on luck to stick with one that has been successful and wish it is not too bad.

The depth of a professional gambler's chips is a huge factor that determines the gambler's strategy. A gambler with a deep pocket can bully the opponent by playing bets with higher risks. However, a shallow-pocketed gambler can't afford such a risk, which leads to defensive play or sometimes one-time, aggressive all-in.

© Rongpeng Li and Aiichiro Nakano 2022
R. Li and A. Nakano, *Simulation with Python*, https://doi.org/10.1007/978-1-4842-8185-7_3

Random Pick and Naive Greedy Approach

Now, let's think about the more general cases and formulate the problem mathematically.

Suppose we have K machines and we use i to index them. Each machine's probability of winning is denoted by p_i. For simplicity, different values of p_i can be assumed, so there are no equivalent machines. What we want to achieve is that after all N pulls, we have the highest expected times of winning.

What is the ideal case? Of course, we want to play the machine with the highest probability of winning $p^* = max\,(p_i)$ if we know which it is. Given this ideal case, we can define a so-called regret function:

$$r = Np^* - \sum_{t=1}^{N} p(t)$$

Here, $p(t)$ is the probability of winning of the machine that Bob plays at timestep t. If we can identify the optimal machine and stick to it, we will have no regret at all which yields $r = 0$. However, if we play the worst machine all the time, the largest possible value of the regret function will be $r = N(p^* - min\,(p_i))$. In Bob's case, $N = 100$ and $K = 3$.

Let's establish a baseline for the regret function. Let's say Bob is a simple man, so he plays the game with one of the two simple strategies:

1. Bob picks a machine randomly each time regardless of the performances.

2. Bob plays each machine ten times and calculates the winning probabilities. He then sticks to the one with highest probabilities of winning and updates the statistics according to the result of play. In other words, Bob is *greedy*.

Let's simulate this bold strategy with winning probability $p_1 = 0.5$, $p_2 = 0.3$, $p_3 = 0.2$:

```
def cal_simple_random_regret(N = 100, probs = [0.5, 0.3, 0.2]):
    regret = max(probs)*N - sum(np.random.choice(probs) for t in range(N)
    return regret
cal_simple_random_regret()
```

The value of the regret function is about *14.6* for my first try. Let's check the distribution of the results for 1000 trials:

```
trials = 1000
with plt.xkcd():
    fig, ax = plt.subplots(figsize=(8,6))
    plt.hist([cal_simple_random_regret() for _ in
    range(trials)],label="Regret value",bins=20)
    ax.set_title("Distribution of Regret Function \n with Random Slot
    Machine Choice",fontsize=20)
    plt.legend()
    fig.savefig("random_slot_machine.jpg")
```

The distribution looks like the graph shown in Figure 3-1.

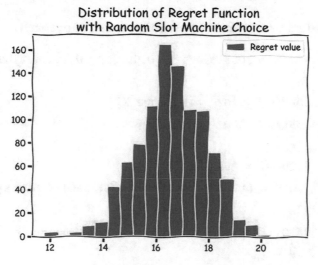

Figure 3-1. *Regret function distribution for random choice*

It looks like the regret value is around *16.5*.

Now, let's examine our second strategy: Bob sticks to the machine with the highest probability of winning after the initial 30 pulls which estimate the winning probabilities. This strategy focuses on the *exploitation* of the known best after an initial *exploration* stage.

First, I will define a *dataclass* called *Record* that stores the information of each machine's record:

```
from dataclasses import dataclass
@dataclass
class Record:
    total:int
    win:int

    def cal_ratio(self):
        return self.win/self.total

    def update(self, prob):
        self.total += 1
        self.win += np.random.random() < prob
```

Then we calculate the regret function with the greedy approach:

```
def cal_greedy_regret(N = 100, probs = [0.5, 0.3, 0.2], evaluation_step = 10):
    K = len(probs)
    Records = [Record(0,0) for _ in range(K)]
    # initial evaluation step
    for i in range(K):
        Records[i].total = evaluation_step
        Records[i].win = np.sum([np.random.random() < probs[i] for _ in
        range(10)])
    # get the index of the most successful slot machine so far
    slots_trajectory = []
    slot_index = np.argmax([record.cal_ratio() for record in Records])
    slots_trajectory.append(slot_index)
    for i in range(N - evaluation_step * K):
        # play the remaining 70 rounds
        Records[slot_index].update(probs[slot_index])
        slot_index = np.argmax([record.cal_ratio() for record in Records])
        slots_trajectory.append(slot_index)
    # print(Records)
    return max(probs)*N - sum([Records[i].total*probs[i] for i in
    range(K)]), slots_trajectory
```

Here, I return both the regret value and the slot machine trajectory, which is the last 70 choices of the slot machines.

If you run this code, you will see a typical regret value of 5. The reader can pause and think about the reason.

There is a big chance that during the exploration stage the first slot machine is going to give you a higher probability of winning than the second and the third, so we start with the first slot machine and stick with it. This way, we will play on slot machine *1* for *80* times and slot machines *2* and *3* for *10* times each. So the regret value is

$$r = 0.5 * 100 - 0.5 * 80 - 0.3 * 10 - 0.2 * 10 = 5.$$

However, sometimes the regret value can be high because the slot machine with the highest probability of winning is not the one we stick to. You can find *slot_trajectory* like the following one. I just plotted one out for you in Figure 3-2.

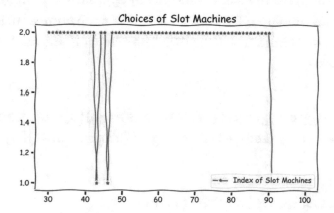

Figure 3-2. *Slot machine choices*

In this case, slot machine *2* gives Bob a good impression during the exploration stage so Bob sticks with it. However, during the exploitation stage, the true best slot machine *1* tries to steal Bob's favor but not successfully. Then Bob stays with slot machine *2* for the majority of the rest of the game. Such a trajectory gives Bob a regret value of *16.8* which is even slightly worse than random guess.

The situation can be worse if Bob doesn't want to spend 30 dollars on exploring/ estimating the probabilities. This way, there is a bigger chance that Bob picks suboptimal slot machines.

The question now is to find an improved version of the greedy approach to avoid such issues.

Greedy-Epsilon: Greedy but Not Always

Let's try to introduce a new strategy. Suppose Bob largely sticks to the best one according to *history*. However, each time Bob has a small chance, denoted by $\in$, he will randomly pick another slot machine to play. This is a mixture of *exploration* and *exploitation*: Bob gives up some opportunity to *exploit* but to *explore*, in search of bigger future gain.

The implementation is straightforward and left to readers as an exercise. Please name the function cal_greedy_epsilon_regret. The key lines are the following three lines. The value of $\in$ is up to you, while I set it to be 0.02 for our demo.

```
if np.random.random() < epsilon:
    slot_index = np.random.choice([i for i in range(K) if i != slot_index])
slots_trajectory.append(slot_index)
```

Let's compare the performances of pure greedy approach and the greedy-epsilon approach with limited initial exploration steps. I will set the number of initial exploration to be just *1* for each machine and $\in$ to be *0.02*. The following code will plot a histogram for both approaches:

```
rounds = 1000
greedy_only = [cal_greedy_regret(evaluation_step=1)[0] for _ in range(rounds)]
greedy_epsilon = [cal_greedy_epsilon_regret(epsilon=0.02)[0] for _ in
range(rounds)]
with plt.xkcd():
    fig, ax = plt.subplots(figsize=(10,6))
    plt.hist(greedy_only,label="Greedy Only",bins=np.
    linspace(0,25,30),alpha=0.5)
    plt.hist(greedy_epsilon,label="Greedy Epsilon",bins=np.
    linspace(0,25,30),alpha=0.5)
    plt.legend(loc='upper right')
    fig.savefig("greedy_approach_epsilon_compare.jpg")
```

The result is presented in Figure 3-3.

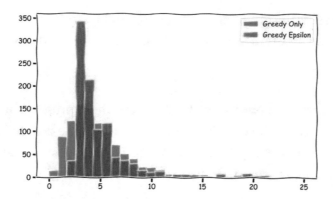

Figure 3-3. *Regret function distribution for pure greedy approach and greedy-epsilon approach*

Note that the pure greedy approach does produce more low regret values, but it is less centralized than the greedy-epsilon approach. This means that the worst cases for greedy approach are worse than the worst cases for greedy-epsilon approach.

The result can be drastically different if you change the ground truth of the winning probabilities. Change it and see how it influences the performance of these two strategies. How about more slot machines like *5* or *10*?

If Bob is aggressive, he will go for a pure greedy approach. If Bob is more cautious, he can try the greedy-epsilon approach to avoid low-probability but catastrophic regret values.

An Improved Greedy-Epsilon Algorithm

One issue with the naive greedy approach is that it doesn't take the slot machine's performance into consideration when making a random choice. We can solve this problem by adopting the so-called *softmax* strategy. The idea is that we introduce a parameter, mimicking the quantity temperature in physics, called τ. The higher the temperature τ is, the more random the choice becomes. At $\tau \approx 0$, our strategy should reduce to the naive greedy approach. At $\tau \approx \infty$, our strategy should reduce to the random choice strategy.

The formula reads as follows:

$$prob_{i,t} = \frac{e^{p_{i,t}/\tau}}{\sum_i e^{p_{i,t}/\tau}}$$

Here, $p_{i,t}$ represents the observed winning probability of slot machine i at time t. For example, if at step *100*, Bob has played slot machine *1* for *11* times and he won *4* times, then $P_{1,100} = \dfrac{4}{100}$.

What does the name *softmax* mean? If we expand the expression in the three slot machine cases and assume the first slot machine performs the best so far, we can then manipulate the value of the temperature τ to see its influence on our next round's pick. For example, when τ approaches infinity, we have the following:

$$prob_{1,t} = \frac{e^{p_{1,t}/\tau}}{e^{p_{1,t}/\tau} + e^{p_{2,t}/\tau} + e^{p_{3,t}/\tau}} \approx \frac{e^0}{e^0 + e^0 + e^0} = \frac{1}{3}$$

This means that at very high temperatures, the algorithm reduces to the baseline random strategy no matter how far slot machine 1 outperforms others.

Let's see another extreme case when the temperature τ is set close to *0*:

$$prob_{1,t} == \frac{1}{1 + e^{(p_{2,t}-p_{1,t})/\tau} + e^{(p_{3,t}-p_{1,t})/\tau}} \approx \frac{1}{1+0+0} = 1$$

Because $p_{1,t}$ is the largest value, expression like $e^{(p_{2,t}-p_{1,t})/\tau}$ essentially becomes $e^{-\infty}$ which is zero. This means our algorithm reduces to the naive greedy approach.

Feel free to tweak the value of τ and see how it affects the performance of the strategy.

The biggest improvement of this strategy is that it will prioritize the best performers but make room for the catch-ups to give a try.

Exercise

1. Try the greedy approach with different numbers of evaluation steps. Try smaller ones like *5* and larger ones like *20*. You may need to run the simulation multiple times to get a statistically consistent result.

2. Study how the true probabilities influence the performance of different strategies. We have been using *probs* = [0.5, 0.3, 0.2] all the time. How about other choices of probabilities?

The Bayesian Way, a Primer on Bayesian Statistics

Now, let's go back to the ideal case that Bob has enough money to keep playing until dawn. How can Bob update his estimation of the winning probabilities of the multiple slot machines while playing? What are our best estimates of the winning probabilities of the multiple slot machines? Can Bob get a *distribution* of their winning probabilities rather than a single value? The answer is *yes*, and Bob needs Bayesian statistics to optimize our estimation.

The core idea in the slot machine context is that Bob will initially hold a belief of the winning probabilities' distributions. Let's say one machine's winning probability p has a distribution called *prior(p)*. Then, Bob will update his belief by observing the actual winning probabilities of the multiple slot machines to get an updated distribution called *posterior(p)*. p is the winning probability being modeled, while the number of winning or losing is the observation. For a given probability, the observation will follow a Binomial distribution. Recall that $Binomial(k, n, p) = \binom{n}{k} p^k (1-p)^{n-k}$ is the probability of observing k successes in an n rounds Binominal experiment with an underlined probability p.

A prior distribution is nothing fancy but a *belief*. Let's say you were born in the United States and believed the United States has the spiciest pepper in the world when you were young. Therefore, $P(U.S.\ has\ spiciest\ pepper) = 1$ was your prior belief. Then you traveled around the world and found that Mexico has pretty spicy pepper. Then your *observation* updates your belief to $P(U.S.\ has\ spiciest\ pepper) = 0.5$. Then you tried some Indian pepper, and your belief changed to $P(U.S.\ has\ spiciest\ pepper) = 0.3$. You keep doing this, and your previous round's belief gets updated as observations come in.

In Bob's case, the observations depend on the parameter p that we keep updating. The update rule is as follows:

$$posterior(p) \approx likelihood(p; x) \times prior(p)$$

Recall that the Bayesian theorem states that for arbitrary events, we have

$$P(A|B) = \frac{P(B|A)P(A)}{P(B)}$$

Mapping this formula to Bob's game, we can see A is essentially the underlying parameter p and B is the pulling result. Since the observations are *fact* that we see, $P(B)$

is independent of our choice of A. Just think of it in Bob's scenario. Bob doesn't care about the winning probability's distribution if he comes from the future and already knows his win or loss, right?

Unfortunately, the Bayesian's updating rule needs to be calculated precisely because we are interested in the exact distribution of p. The Bayesian updating rule is not a simple one, and its computation can be very expensive especially in the continuous case. What we want now is to find a nice-behaving distribution of $prior(p)$ such that the updated is also nice-behaving so the update rule can be computed quickly and sequentially.

Does such a nice prior distribution exist? Yes! It is called a *conjugate prior* of the likelihood distribution. Here, the likelihood function is the Binomial distribution, and its conjugate prior is called the *Beta* distribution parameterized by two parameters, α and β: $B(\alpha, \beta)$.

The Beta distribution is a generalization of the Binomial distribution. Let's take a look at some examples in Figure 3-4.

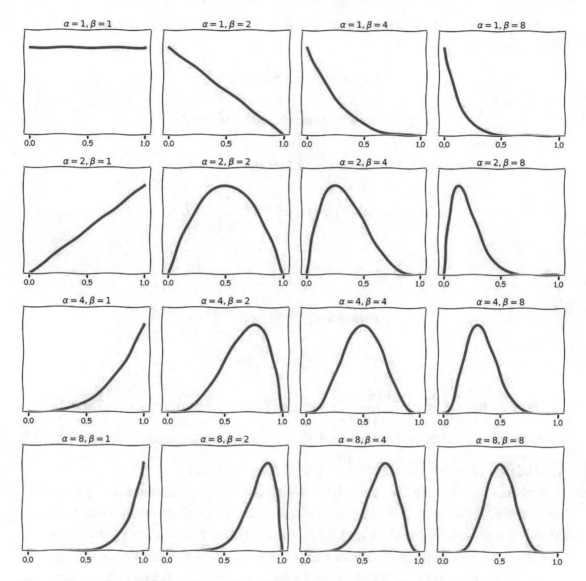

Figure 3-4. *Beta distributions with different sets of parameters*

It is very similar to the Binomial distribution. If α and β are the same, the distribution is symmetric. If both parameters are larger, the distribution is more centric. If α is larger than β, the distribution is left skewed and vice versa.

If we plug in the Beta distribution's formula into the update rule, we get the following result:

$$posterior \approx likelihood \times prior$$

$$posterior \approx Binomial(k;n,p) \times B(p;\alpha,\beta)$$

Expand the expression for Binomial and Beta distributions:

$$posterior \approx \binom{n}{k} p^k (1-p)^{n-k} \times \frac{p^{\alpha-1}(1-p)^{\beta-1}}{B(\alpha,\beta)}$$

$$posterior \approx p^{\alpha-1}(1-p)^{\beta-1} p^k (1-p)^{n-k}$$

$$posterior \approx p^{\alpha+k-1}(1-p)^{\beta+n-k-1}$$

$$posterior \approx B(p;\alpha+k,\beta+n-k)$$

Here, we have $B(\alpha,\beta) = \dfrac{\Gamma(\alpha)\Gamma(\beta)}{\Gamma(\alpha+\beta)}$ where $\Gamma(x)$ is the gamma function. Don't be intimidated because in the case of α and β being integers, gamma function $\Gamma(x)$ is just a factorial $(x-1)!$ which cancels the $\binom{n}{k}$ part in the expression.

Alright, enough math for now. What does it mean in the context of Bob's gambling? It means that if Bob starts with a belief of $B(\alpha,\beta)$, each time if there is a success, he can simply update his belief to $B(\alpha+1,\beta)$, and if there is a loss, he can simply update his belief to $B(\alpha,\beta+1)$. There is no calculation involved at all, just parameter updating!

We have a new question: What value of α and β should Bob choose? This is quite empirical. Bob can compare his historical records with the distributions with different parameters and pick the best one. However, at the end of the day, the initial choice won't matter much. Another practical question is how to decide which machine to play in the next round? Simple! We just use the Beta distributions of the slot machines to generate a set of samples and pick the largest one. The idea is the same as the *softmax* strategy in the previous section.

Let's look at the codes that perform the simulation and visualize the results:

```python
probs = [0.5, 0.3, 0.2]
K = len(probs)
N = 100
rounds = [9, 49, 99]
fig, axis = plt.subplots(1, 3, figsize= (30,10))
x_ticks = np.linspace(0,1,500)
plot_index = 0
betas = [stats.beta(1,1) for _ in range(K)]
wins = [0, 0, 0]
totals = [0, 0, 0]

with plt.xkcd():
    for rnd in range(N):
        for i in range(K):
            betas[i] = stats.beta(1+wins[i],1+totals[i]-wins[i])
        p_value_samples = np.array([betas[i].rvs() for i in range(K)])
        slot_next_round_index = p_value_samples.argmax()
        win = np.random.random() < probs[slot_next_round_index]
        wins[slot_next_round_index] += win
        totals[slot_next_round_index] += 1
        if rnd in rounds:
            ax = axis[plot_index]
            for i in range(K):
                # plotting
                beta = betas[i]
                ax.plot(x_ticks, beta.pdf(x_ticks),
                        label='Bandit {}'.format(i+1),
                        linewidth=3)
                ax.set_title('After {} rounds'.format(rnd + 1),fontsize=20)
                ax.legend(fontsize=20)
            plot_index+=1
```

Figure 3-5 is the visualization of our winning probability distributions. Your result may be different because there is randomness involved.

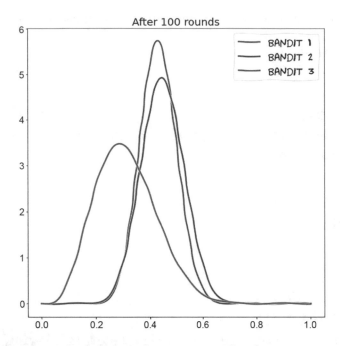

Figure 3-5. *Winning probabilities after 100 rounds of run*

What can we learn from this result? Well, we have a much higher confidence in the winning probability of the machine with the largest winning probability, which is the first one. The reason is that because it has a higher winning probability, Bob has a higher chance of picking it, which creates positive feedback. Also, as Bob plays more and more, we have higher confidence for all machines in general.

Let's try more rounds and try more machines. Let's say Bob has 200 dollars, and there are *4* machines with similar winning probabilities *probs* = [0.8, 0.7, 0.6, 0.5]. The probability estimation is presented in Figure 3-6.

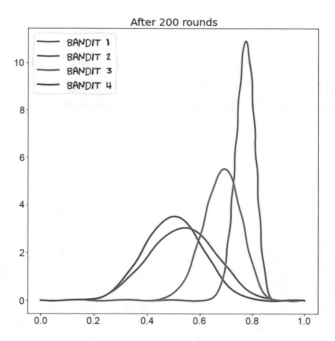

Figure 3-6. *Bandit winning probability estimation after 200 rounds*

It is clear that after 200 rounds, the superior machine is quite obvious, and we can say it with a precise level of confidence.

Exercise

1. Simplify the posterior updating expression on your own.

2. Can you think of a way to combine the *softmax* strategy and the Bayesian strategy? Let's say you use the result of the Bayesian estimation to adjust the temperature of the softmax strategy. Your result doesn't need to be mathematically solid, but it needs to make sense intuitively.

3. Calculate the regret function using the Bayesian approach. Is it significantly better than other strategies?

Summary

In this chapter, we studied an interesting gambling scenario. We demonstrated that different gambling strategies are based on different levels of preference over exploration or exploitation. We also ran the simulation based on the Bayesian approach.

CHAPTER 4

Balls in a 2-D Box, a Simple Physics Engine

If you are a gaming fan or an anime fan, you probably heard about the term physics engine. When you play Kratos in the *God of War*, his axes interact with the enemies and the environment. You feel that such interaction is real, and his axes are indeed heavy and metal-like. What you are actually controlling is just a playstation controller, but the impression is on another level. Here, physics engines are responsible for creating such feelings of being in a physical world.

A physics engine is a computer software that simulates certain physics systems such as rigid-body interaction, fluid dynamics, lighting systems, etc. In video games, physics engines are responsible for simulating the interaction of players with the environment. If players destroy a building, the collapsing of the building has to be like in real life: bricks are heavy, and wooden structures are light. In animation like *Moana*, the water effect is created by physics engines that are dedicated to simulate water movement. There are physics engines designed for snowflakes, hairs, and other systems as well.

In this chapter, we are going to build our own simplistic physics engine to simulate a very limited system: balls in a 2-D box.

One Ball in a 2-D Box

Let's start with the simplest example. The scenario is very much like pooling or snooker, but we will start with only one ball. The following code snippet draws a ball in the middle of a rectangular box:

```
RADIUS = 0.2
POSITION = [1,1]
VELOCITY = [0.2, 0.2]
```

© Rongpeng Li and Aiichiro Nakano 2022
R. Li and A. Nakano, *Simulation with Python*, https://doi.org/10.1007/978-1-4842-8185-7_4

```
WIDTH, HEIGHT = 10, 8
ARROW_HEAD_WIDTH, ARROW_HEAD_LENGTH = 0.05, 0.2

with plt.xkcd():
    fig, ax = plt.subplots(figsize=(WIDTH, HEIGHT))
    plt.xlim(0,WIDTH)
    plt.ylim(0,HEIGHT)
    ball_1 = plt.Circle(POSITION, RADIUS, color='r')
    ax.add_patch(ball_1)
    ax.arrow(*POSITION,
             *VELOCITY,
             head_width=ARROW_HEAD_WIDTH,
             head_length=ARROW_HEAD_LENGTH,
             fc='k', ec='k')
    plt.plot()
```

The visualization in Figure 4-1 clearly shows the position, size, and velocity of the ball. Note that the ball is moving up with a velocity indicated by the arrow.

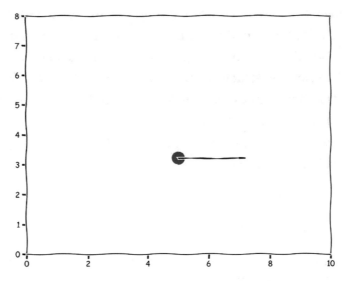

Figure 4-1. *A single ball moving to the right*

What exactly do we mean by velocity of *(0.2, 0.2)*? Let's define some concrete units for our simulation. Let's say the lengths are in meters and time is in seconds. Therefore, the velocity of the ball is in meters per second. Our ball starts at position *(0.2, 0.2)* and is heading top right with an approximate speed of 0.28 meters per second.

What I described is the physical setting up which means in the real world such a ball will move continuously. However, simulations are discrete, and we need to define the *timestep*, denoted by Δt, to approximate the continuous motion in reality. A *timestep* is the amount of time that passes between two consecutive steps of the simulation.

The smaller the Δt is, the more *frames* we get per second. For example, if the timestep is 0.1 seconds, we will have *10* frames per second (fps). For each frame, the ball will move 0.1*0.28=0.028 meters. If the timestep is 0.01 seconds, we will have 100 frames per second (fps). For each frame, the ball will move 0.01*0.28=0.0028 meters. In gaming, if the fps is above 60, players usually won't detect any glitches in the game. In movie animation, if the fps is above 24, the animation will look smooth.

However, high fps also demands more computation to calculate the positions, facings, rotations, and velocities of objects. In our one-ball case, we can pick a timestep of 0.1 second. For a simulation of 1 second, our computer will need to update the position of the ball ten times.

The time in the simulated system is different from the time in the real world. In order to simulate one second in the simulated system, the computer may run up for hours if the system is complicated. For gaming, this is even not acceptable. There are *game engines* that liberate game developers from the burden of working against the *physics engine* directly. One such example is the *Unreal Engine*.

Physics Law of Motion

Let's simplify our system a little bit first. We assume the following conditions:

1. There is no friction in the system. The ball will not slow down due to friction with air or other objects.

2. There is no rotation in the system. The ball will not rotate. If you play table tennis, you will know that rotation makes a huge difference in the game.

3. The collisions are elastic. Elastic collision means that the ball will not lose energy when it collides with the walls of the box. If there are multiple balls, as we will see in the next section, the colliding balls as a whole will not lose energy.

4. Gravity is not present in the system. The ball will not fall down due to gravity. However, we will remove this restriction very soon.

Given such simplifications, we can write the following update rules of our system according to Newton's laws of motion:

$$x_{t+1} = x_t + \upsilon_t * \Delta t$$

$$\upsilon_{t+1} = \upsilon_t + a_t * \Delta t$$

Since we assume there are no external forces, the acceleration a_t initially is 0. Now, let's update our system by simulating the motion for ten iterations with a timestep of 0.2 seconds and velocity of (2,2). The code for performing the simulation is as follows. They are just two simple functions:

```
def render(pos = POSITION, vel = VELOCITY):
    with plt.xkcd():
        fig, ax = plt.subplots(figsize=(WIDTH, HEIGHT))
        plt.xlim(0,WIDTH)
        plt.ylim(0,HEIGHT)
        ball_1 = plt.Circle(pos, RADIUS, color='r')
        ax.add_patch(ball_1)
        ax.arrow(*pos,
                  *vel,
                  head_width=ARROW_HEAD_WIDTH,
                  head_length=ARROW_HEAD_LENGTH,
                  fc='k', ec='k')
        plt.show()

def update(pos=POSITION, vel = VELOCITY, acc = None, delta_t = DELTA_T):
    # Note that all values are mutable so the update is in place
    for i in range(len(pos)):
        pos[i] += vel[i] * delta_t
    if acc:
        for i in range(len(pos)):
            vel[i] += acc[i] * delta_t
```

Now, we can use our preset parameters to perform the simulation:

```
RADIUS = 0.2
POSITION = [1,1]
VELOCITY = [2,2]
WIDTH, HEIGHT = 10, 8
ARROW_HEAD_WIDTH, ARROW_HEAD_LENGTH = 0.05, 0.2
DELTA_T = 0.2

render(pos=POSITION, vel = VELOCITY)
for _ in range(10):
    update(pos=POSITION, vel = VELOCITY,delta_t = DELTA_T)
    render(pos=POSITION, vel = VELOCITY)
```

Let's see where the ball is after ten iterations in Figure 4-2.

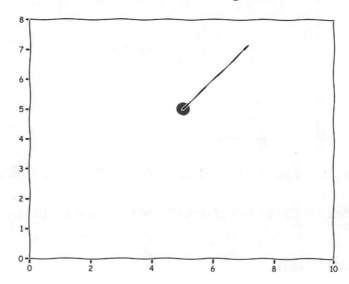

Figure 4-2. *The ball's position and velocity after ten iterations*

As expected, for ten iterations with a timestep of 0.2 seconds, the system evolves for 2 seconds. With a velocity of (2,2), the ball will move 4 meters in both the horizontal and vertical directions.

Now, let's add some gravity to the system to get rid of the last assumptions we had earlier. The modification is quite simple. To keep the ball in the box for the first several frames, I have set the acceleration to be 1 meter per second squared downward. The normal gravity acceleration on earth is about *9.8* meters per second squared.

```
ACCELERATION = [0,-1]
for _ in range(10):
    update(pos=POSITION, vel = VELOCITY, acc = ACCELERATION, delta_t =
    DELTA_T)
    render(pos=POSITION, vel = VELOCITY)
```

Let's do a back-of-the-envelope calculation of the velocity. After 2 seconds, the ball will lose all its speed in the vertical direction, so the velocity vector should be purely horizontal. Let's check in Figure 4-3.

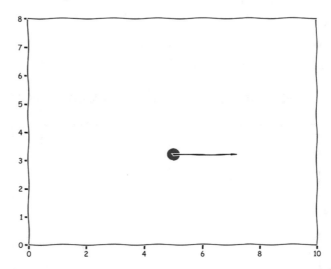

Figure 4-3. *Ball's position and velocity after 2 seconds in gravity field*

As expected, the ball completely loses its speed in the vertical direction.

Collision Detection

Now, let's tackle the elephant in the room, handling the collision detection.

To detect something, we need a clear definition of collision. What does it mean to have a collision between a wall and a ball? The idea is simple: if the ball's center of geometry is at a shorter distance than the radius against the wall, then there is a collision. This is clearly illustrated in Figure 4-4.

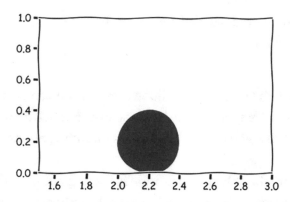

Figure 4-4. *Zoom-in of a collision*

The logic of detection becomes simple: if at a timestamp, the distance between the center of the ball and either wall is less than the radius of the ball, then there is a collision. For the next iteration, the ball will bounce off the wall by flipping the sign of the corresponding velocity components. The system then evolves from there.

Let's introduce a function to check possible collisions between the ball and the walls: if the ball is still moving toward the wall and the distance is already less than the radius, then a collision is detected. The function will also flip the sign of corresponding velocity components if a collision is detected.

```
def detect_collision_wall(pos = POSITION, vel = VELOCITY, radius = RADIUS,
height = HEIGHT, width = WIDTH):
    # left wall
    if abs(pos[0]-0) < radius and vel[0] < 0:
        vel[0] = - vel[0]
        return
    # right wall
    if abs(width-pos[0])< radius and vel[0] > 0:
        vel[0] = -vel[0]
        return
    # upper wall
    if abs(height-pos[1]) < radius and vel[1] > 0:
        vel[1] = -vel[1]
        return
    # lower wall
```

```
if abs(pos[1]-0) < radius and vel[1] < 0:
    vel[1] = -vel[1]
    return
```

You may notice that the collision condition depends on an assumption that the ball is moving at a *moderate* speed. If the ball is so fast that between two neighboring frames, the ball passes through the wall, known as *tunneling* problem, then the collision detection will never be triggered.

Another issue is that the collision condition is lagging behind the actual motion of the ball. This can be mitigated by introducing a small positive parameter called *delta* to turn the distance calculation between the ball and wall into something like *abs(pos[0]-0) < radius + delta*.

By picking a proper value of *delta*, depending on the velocity of the ball or distribution of speeds for multiple-ball simulations, we can reduce the effect of lagging.

Now, let's take a look at the simulated system to see how the ball bounces.

Figure 4-5 shows the direction our red ball is heading to.

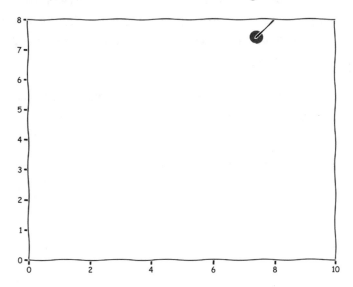

Figure 4-5. *A ball is heading toward a collision*

After the collision, the ball changes direction. Our algorithm works fine!

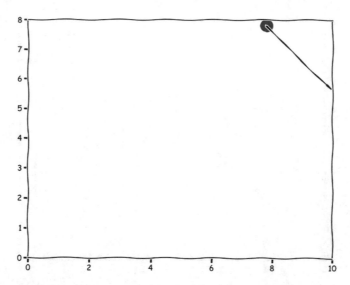

Figure 4-6. *Velocity of the ball changes right after the collision*

Let's take a quick look to see how to create a gif animation before moving on.

You can use the *imageio* Python library to create a gif animation. Let's say you have saved the snapshot of the system to files *1.png, 2.png, 3.png,* etc. You can use the following command to create a gif animation:

```
import imageio
filenames = ["1.png", "2.png","3.png"]
with imageio.get_writer('one_ball_bounce.gif', mode='I') as writer:
    for filename in filenames:
        image = imageio.imread(filename)
        writer.append_data(image)
```

For the one-ball case, the animation looks like the one in GIF 4-1.

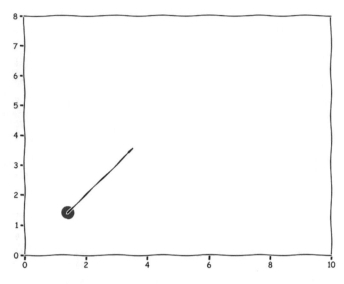

GIF 4-1. *Ball's movement without gravity*

If we add gravity to the system, the animation will look like the one in GIF 4-2.

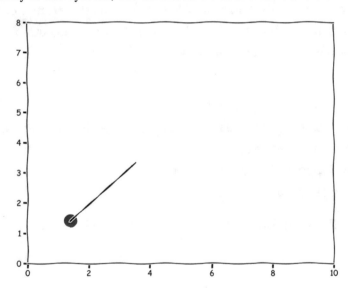

GIF 4-2. *Ball's movement with gravity*

Already very cool, isn't it?

Exercise

1. Introduce the *delta* to the simulation. What is the relationship between the speed of the ball and the value of *delta*?

2. Can you increase the frame rate (fps) of the animation? Does it look more realistic?

Multiple Balls in a 2-D Box

Now, let's talk about the case of multiple balls. Besides the possibility of wall-ball collision, we can also have collisions between balls. This introduces two new problems:

1. How to detect the collision between balls?

2. How do balls behave when they collide?

If you think about the first problem, if there are 100 balls in a box, then theoretically the between-ball collision is a n^2 operation like in the thousands, naively. This becomes unhandleable, therefore unacceptable, quickly. You don't want the magnitude of calculation to grow quadratically. However, since the majority of balls won't have a chance to collide with each other, we may want to use a more efficient algorithm to detect or predict the collision between balls.

Let's solve the second problem first. It seems easier compared to the first one, isn't it?

Update of Positions and Velocity upon Collision

There are two physics laws that govern the movement of purely elastic balls: the law of conservation of momentum and the law of conservation of energy. In the simulation of wall-ball collision, we assume the wall has infinite mass so the momentum of the ball is forcefully reversed by the wall while preserving the energy of the ball. Since the ball's energy is the sum of kinetic energy and potential energy, if we introduce gravity, the speed of the ball is unchanged.

For the ball-ball collision, things become a little bit uncomplicated. We are not going to deduce the formulas in detail, but we can do some back-of-the-envelope analysis after checking the formulas.

Let's denote the center of the two balls as c_1 and c_2, the radius of the two balls as r_1 and r_2, and the velocity of the two balls as v_1 and v_2. We will use the prime notation v_1' and v_2' to denote the velocities of the balls after the collision. Different from the case of wall-ball collision, we also need to consider the masses of the two balls. This agrees with our intuition because even a fast ping-pong ball is not going to move a golf ball much. Let's call them m_1 and m_2.

Now, the two physics laws that govern the motion are listed as follows: the conservation of momentum and the conservation of energy.

$$m_1 v_1 + m_2 v_2 = m_1 v_1' + m_2 v_2'$$

$$\frac{1}{2} m_1 v_1'^2 + \frac{1}{2} m_2 v_2'^2 = \frac{1}{2} m_1 v_1^2 + \frac{1}{2} m_2 v_2^2$$

Note that all the velocities are vectors rather than scalars. For example, v_1 has two components $v_1[0]$ and $v_1[1]$ and v_2 has two components $v_2[0]$ and $v_2[1]$, etc. Since the only two quantities we don't know are v_1' and v_2', we can rearrange the equations to obtain them. This is a great mathematical exercise and is left to the reader as an exercise. For now, I will offer you the solutions:

$$v_1' = v_1 - \frac{2m_2}{m_1 + m_2} \frac{<v_1 - v_2, c_1 - c_2>}{\|c_1 - c_2\|^2} (c_1 - c_2)$$

$$v_2' = v_2 - \frac{2m_1}{m_1 + m_2} \frac{<v_2 - v_1, c_2 - c_1>}{\|c_1 - c_2\|^2} (c_2 - c_1)$$

Let's get a visual impression of what's going on and write a function to compute the post-collision velocities. Assume that two balls are colliding into each other as illustrated in Figure 4-7.

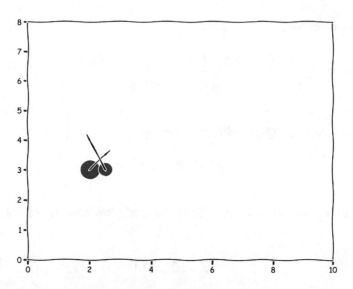

Figure 4-7. *Two balls colliding into each other*

We assume that the balls are so hard that the distance between two centers is always exactly the sum of their radii. I have picked the parameters for these two balls as shown in Table 4-1.

Table 4-1. *Parameters for two balls'*
position, radius, velocity, and masses

v_1	$(0.5, 0.5)$
v_2	$(-0.5, 1)$
r_1	0.3
r_2	0.2
c_1	$(2,3)$
c_2	$(2.5, 3)$
m_1	2
m_2	2

Let's do the calculation then:

$$v_1' = v_1 - \frac{2m_2}{m_1 + m_2} \frac{<v_1 - v_2, c_1 - c_2>}{\|c_1 - c_2\|^2} (c_1 - c_2)$$

Substitute the numbers:

$$v_1' = (0.5,\ 0.5) - \frac{2*3}{2+3} \frac{<(0.5,\ 0.5)-(-0.5,\ 1),(2,\ 3)-(2.5,\ 3)>}{\|(2,\ 3)-(2.5,\ 3)\|^2}((2,\ 3)-(2.5,\ 3))$$

We obtain the first ball's post-collision velocity:

$$v_1' = (-0.7,\ 0.5)$$

By the same token, we can calculate the post-collision velocity of ball 2. The velocity is

$$v_2' = (0.3,\ 1)$$

Visually, the velocity vectors are presented in Figure 4-8.

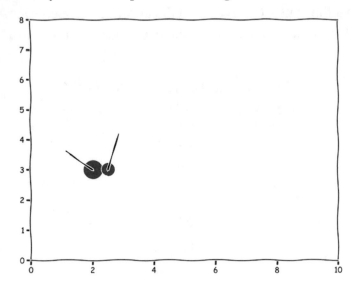

Figure 4-8. *Post-collision velocity of two balls*

Does our result agree with the conservation of momentum and energy? This verification is left to the readers as an exercise.

Now, let's rewrite our rendering function to handle multiple balls. Also, it is time to rewrite our code to represent the objects like balls and boxes into objects and encapsulate the collision logics. I didn't do this earlier because I want the mathematics to be clear and easy to understand. By doing it now, we can make the next section of our tutorial clean and concise.

First, let's create the _box_, _ball_, and _system_ classes. We create them as a *dataclass* because we want to make use of the automatically generated methods such as *__init__* and *__repr__*. The *Box* class is the simplest one.

```
from dataclasses import dataclass
@dataclass
class Box:
    height: float
    width: float
```

Next, we create the *Ball* class in which we implement the main logic of the collision handling. Note that this is no more than a direct translation of the mathematical formulas earlier.

```
@dataclass
class Ball:
    pos: [float, float]
    vel: [float, float]
    mass: float
    radius: float

    def update(self, acc = None, delta_t = 0.2) -> None:
        for i in range(len(self.pos)):
            self.pos[i] += self.vel[i] * delta_t
        if acc:
            for i in range(len(self.pos)):
                self.vel[i] += acc[i] * delta_t

    def detect_ball_collision(self, other) -> None:
        distance = np.sqrt((self.pos[0] - other.pos[0])**2 + (self.pos[1] -
        other.pos[1])**2)
        if self.radius + other.radius >= distance:
            self.ball_collision_update(other)

    def ball_collision_update(self, other)-> None:
        '''
```

```
        Implement the ball collision logic, making use of symmetry.

        ball_1: self
        ball_2: other

        '''

        mass_factor_1 = 2*other.mass/(self.mass + other.mass)
        mass_factor_2 = 2*self.mass/(self.mass + other.mass)

        velocity_diff = [self.vel[0] - other.vel[0], self.vel[1] -
        other.vel[1]]
        center_diff = [self.pos[0] - other.pos[0], self.pos[1] -
        other.pos[1]]
        squared_center_diff = sum([diff**2 for diff in center_diff])

        velocity_factor = np.dot(velocity_diff, center_diff)/squared_
        center_diff <1>

        self.vel[0] -= mass_factor_1 * velocity_factor * center_diff[0]
        self.vel[1] -= mass_factor_1 * velocity_factor * center_diff[1]

        other.vel[0] += mass_factor_2 * velocity_factor * center_diff[0]
        other.vel[1] += mass_factor_2 * velocity_factor * center_diff[1]

    def detect_box_collision(self, box: Box) -> None:
        # left wall
        if abs(self.pos[0]-0) < self.radius and self.vel[0] < 0:
            self.vel[0] = -self.vel[0]
            return
        # right wall
        if abs(box.width-self.pos[0])< self.radius and self.vel[0] > 0:
            self.vel[0] = -self.vel[0]
            return
        # upper wall
        if abs(box.height-self.pos[1]) < self.radius and self.vel[1] > 0:
            self.vel[1] = -self.vel[1]
            return
        # lower wall
```

```
        if abs(self.pos[1]-0) < self.radius and self.vel[1] < 0:
            self.vel[1] = -self.vel[1]
            return
```

The last part is the *System* class. It is a container for the *Box* and *Ball* classes and governs the interaction between them. We also bundle some helpful functions into it like rendering, etc.

```
from typing import List

@dataclass
class System:
    box: Box
    balls: List[Ball]
    acc: float = None
    delta_t: float = 0.2

    def init_balls(self):
        raise NotImplementedError

    def update(self):
        # ball-ball collision detection
        for idx_1 in range(0, len(self.balls)-1):
            for idx_2 in range(idx_1 + 1, len(self.balls)):
                self.balls[idx_1].detect_ball_collision(self.balls[idx_2])

        # ball-wall collision detection
        for ball in self.balls:
            ball.detect_box_collision(self.box)

        # update velocity
        for ball in self.balls:
            ball.update(self.acc, self.delta_t)

    def render(self, save= False, file_name = None, return_array = False):
        with plt.xkcd():
            fig, ax = plt.subplots(figsize=(self.box.width, self.box.height))
            if return_array:
```

```
                from matplotlib.backends.backend_agg import FigureCanvasAgg
                canvas =  FigureCanvasAgg(fig)
            ax.set_xlim(0,self.box.width)
            ax.set_ylim(0,self.box.height)
            for ball in self.balls:
                pos, vel, radius = ball.pos, ball.vel, ball.radius
                ball_patch = plt.Circle(pos, radius, color='r')
                ax.add_patch(ball_patch)
                ax.arrow(*pos,
                        *vel,
                        fc='k', ec='k')
            if save:
                plt.savefig("{}.png".format(file_name))
            if return_array:
                # Retrieve a view on the renderer buffer
                canvas.draw()
                buf = canvas.buffer_rgba()
                # convert to a NumPy array
                return np.asarray(buf)
    def generate_gif(self, file_name = "multiple_ball_collision.gif",
    steps = 100):
        with imageio.get_writer(file_name, mode='I') as writer:
            for _ in range(steps):
                system.update()
                image = system.render(return_array = True)
                writer.append_data(image)
```

Let's take a look at how our two-ball system evolves in GIF 4-3. If you are reading a hard copy, make sure to check online for the animation.

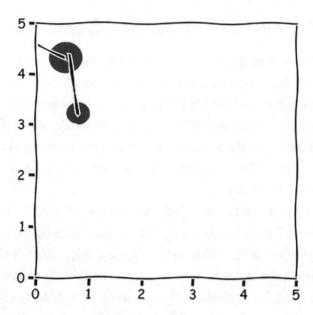

GIF 4-3. *Two balls moving in a box with collisions*

We can also generate a bunch of random balls and see how they evolve as in GIF 4-4. The implementation of this experiment is left to the readers as an exercise. Here is a five-ball system. Notice that the sizes of the balls are not proportional to the mass. Can you guess which ball has the largest mass?

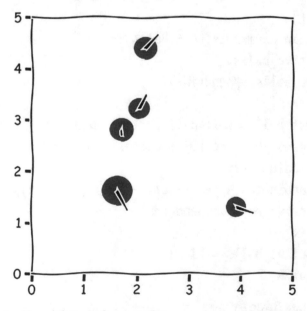

GIF 4-4. *Multiple balls with random radii, masses, and velocities in a box*

Collision Detection in Multiple-Ball Scenario

Now, let's address the elephant in the room: the performance issue of collision detection. There are many well-established collision detection algorithms; we will discuss and implement one of the most intuitive algorithms: the *sweep and prune* algorithm.

The idea of sweep and prune algorithm is quite straightforward. If two balls collide, then their projection in either the x axis or the y axis must collide as well! Therefore, we can use the projection of the balls to predict if they collide or not as it is a necessary, although not sufficient, condition.

The best part of sweep and prune is that we can sort the balls by their projections in one axis beforehand. Then a single sweep can find all pairs that can potentially collide. Sorting is a process of time complexity $O(n \log (n))$, which is already a drastic improvement over the naive approach. An improvement can be made utilizing

Now, let's implement the algorithm. We only need to implement one new method in the *System* class, which is solely responsible for returning a list of pairs of balls that can potentially collide.

```
def sweep_prune(self)-> List[Tuple[int, int]]:
    # return a list of indices of balls that may collide
    self.balls.sort(key = lambda ball: ball.pos[0]) <1>
    active_balls = []
    candidates = []
    for idx, ball in enumerate(self.balls):
        if not active_balls:
            active_balls.append(idx)
        else:
            closest_ball = self.balls[active_balls[-1]]
            if closest_ball.pos[0] + closest_ball.radius >= ball.pos[0] -
            ball.radius: <2>
                candidates.append((active_balls[-1],idx))
                active_balls.append(idx)
            else: <3>
                active_balls = [idx]
    return candidates
```

The algorithm does three things:

1. The balls are sorted in place by their x coordinate.

2. If two balls are close enough in the x axis, then they are candidates
    for collision.

3. Otherwise, empty the *active_balls* list and add the current ball to
    the *active_balls* list, as we move away from the previous cluster of
    ball projections.

Another small place we need to change is in the *update* method in the *System* class:
use *sweep_prune* to select candidates.

```
def update(self):
    # ball-ball collision detection
    candidates = self.sweep_prune()
    for pair_idx in candidates:
            self.balls[pair_idx[0]].detect_ball_collision(self.balls[pair_
            idx[1]])
    # everything else is the same
```

Now, go ahead and try to run the simulation. Notice that if you disable the rendering,
the simulation will run faster. Rendering probably takes much longer than detecting
collisions in our case.

With that, we have reached the end of the chapter. Give it a try to finish the exercises
before moving on to the next chapter.

Exercise

1. Deduce the expression post-collision velocities from the
    conservation of energy and momentum in 2-D. Use another set of
    parameters to verify that the post-collision velocity calculations
    are in agreement with the conservation of momentum and energy.

2. Write a program that confines the total kinetic energy of a 20-ball
    system to a given value. Verify that the kinetic energy remains the
    same during the whole simulation.

3. Add gravity to the five-ball system.

4. What if every collision with the wall will result in an energy loss? Let's say *10%* of the kinetic energy will be lost in each box-wall collision; run a simulation and check what the system looks like.

Summary

In this chapter, we discussed the exciting topic of simulating physics rules. We implemented an algorithm to detect collisions and derived formulas to calculate the post-collision velocities of balls in a 2-D system. We also implemented a more efficient collision detection algorithm for multiple-ball cases.

CHAPTER 5

Percolation, Threshold, and Phase Change

A scientist is investigating the spreading of wildfire in a forest. She is looking for a simple model that can predict how large a wildfire will be given limited knowledge about the forests, the weather, the climate, etc. For example, if some irresponsible tourist dropped a cigarette somewhere in the forest, what is the expectation of the worst-case size of the fire? How about the average size?

Another scientist is studying the robustness of a computer network. He is looking for solutions for disaster recovery under extreme cases. Suppose the network goes down and the administrator only has limited resources to start certain key nodes. How much can the network be restored? Which nodes should be started first given limited resources?

These two questions seem unrelated, but they are actually strongly similar under the name of *percolation*. Percolation or percolation theory is the study of clustering behaviors of random networks. The theory originated naturally from many physical, chemical, and biological systems. For example, in the case of the movement of water in porous material, whether the water can percolate through the porous material depends on the porosity of the material. For medical delivery in muscle tissues, the movement of medical products can also be modeled as a percolation process.

Back to the forest fire questions, if we assume that the forest is a network of trees that between-tree fire spreading is determined by a probability, then the question of forest fire prevention becomes the determination of a critical probability of fire spreading in a percolation process. For the network restoration problem, the percentage of nodes that can be started first is also modelable as a critical probability.

Intuitively, different nodes will have different importance in a network, so we are simplifying the network case strongly now. A better modeling of a network is a graph as we shall revisit in a later chapter.

© Rongpeng Li and Aiichiro Nakano 2022
R. Li and A. Nakano, *Simulation with Python*, https://doi.org/10.1007/978-1-4842-8185-7_5

Now, let's get down to the fundamentals of the percolation theory and run some basic simulations.

Problem Introduction

Clustering behavior can happen on any kind of network in, theoretically, any dimension. The most intuitive one to visualize is the 2-D case as in Figure 5-1. For simplicity, let's assume that the network is a square grid/lattice.

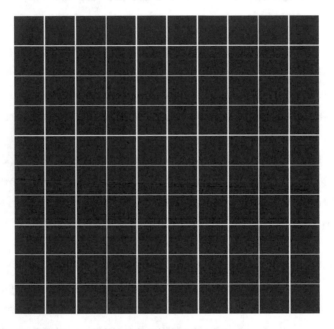

Figure 5-1. *A square lattice of dimension 10 by 10*

What you see in Figure 5-1 is a square grid with size 10 by 10. Let's call each red square a site, then this finite grid has 100 sites. Each site can have two states, either occupied or unoccupied. In our forest fire case, the tree can be either burning or safe. Now, I am assigning a blue color to the occupied sites and redrawing the grid. I can also use a bond to connect the adjacent occupied sites. One typical state of the grid looks like Figure 5-2.

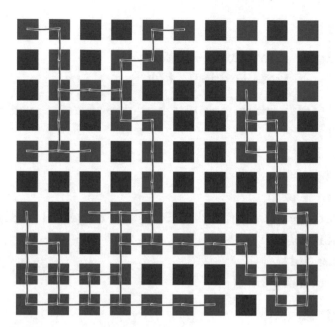

Figure 5-2. *Grid with occupied sites connected*

Note that I also shrunk the site size so you can see the bonds more clearly. We call the connected occupied sites a cluster. In the preceding case, there is one large cluster that spans almost the entire grid except the three on the top right.

As you can imagine for the forest fire case, this indicates a fire that starts somewhere and spreads to the entire grid. However, there are also some small random fires on the top-right corner that only burned down one isolated tree each.

The example we just showed is a site percolation problem. There is another type called bond percolation problem where the connectivity is measured by linking bonds, rather than sites. For simplicity, we will only focus on the site percolation problem in this chapter. The bond percolation problem simulation is left to the readers as an exercise.

Before moving on, I would like to show you how the Grid class is defined and how the grid is rendered:

```
from enum import Enum

class State(Enum):
    Working = 1
    Broken = 0
```

```python
class Grid:

    state_to_color = {State.Broken: "red",
                      State.Working: "blue"}

    def __init__(self, width = WIDTH, height = HEIGHT, prob = PROB, random_
    init = False):
        self.width = width
        self.height = height
        self.prob = prob
        self.states = [[State.Broken for _ in range(self.height)] for _ in
        range(self.width)]
        if random_init:
            self.random_init()

    def random_init(self):
        for w in range(self.width):
            for h in range(self.height):
                if np.random.uniform() < self.prob:
                    self.states[w][h] = State.Working

    def render(self, return_array = False, block_size = 1300):
        with plt.xkcd():
            fig, ax = plt.subplots(figsize=(self.width+1, self.height+1))
            if return_array:
                from matplotlib.backends.backend_agg import FigureCanvasAgg
                canvas = FigureCanvasAgg(fig)
            ax.set_xlim(0,self.width+1)
            ax.set_ylim(0,self.height+1)
            ax.axis('off')
            # draw the sites
            x, y, c = [], [], []

            # Note that w,h are for plotting coordinates.
            for w in range(1,self.width+1):
                for h in range(1,self.height+1):
                    x.append(w)
                    y.append(h)
```

```
            state = self.states[w-1][h-1]
            c.append(Grid.state_to_color[state])

plt.scatter(x, y, c = c, marker="s", s = block_size)

# draw the bonds between working site
# from bottom left, expand up and right to connect
for w in range(1,self.width):
    for h in range(1,self.height):
        origin_state = self.states[w-1][h-1]
        if origin_state == State.Working:
            up_state = self.states[w-1][h]
            if up_state == State.Working:
                plt.plot((w, w), (h, h+1), c = Grid.state_to_
                color[State.Working])
            right_state = self.states[w][h-1]
            if right_state == State.Working:
                plt.plot( (w, w+1), (h, h), c = Grid.state_to_
                color[State.Working])

# top line
for w in range(1,self.width):
    origin_state = self.states[w-1][self.height-1]
    right_state = self.states[w][self.height-1]
    if origin_state == State.Working and right_state == State.
    Working:
        plt.plot((w,w+1),(self.height,self.height), c = Grid.
        state_to_color[State.Working])

# right line
for h in range(1,self.height):
    origin_state = self.states[self.width - 1][h-1]
    up_state = self.states[self.width - 1][h]
    if origin_state == State.Working and up_state == State.
    Working:
        plt.plot((self.width,self.width),(h,h+1), c = Grid.
        state_to_color[State.Working])
```

Now, let's get down to the key question. Given a varying occupation probability p and independence between sites (or bonds), when will a cluster percolate through our grid from the top edge to the bottom edge?

Percolation and the Critical Probability

Well, mathematicians are more interested in another question: When will an infinite cluster form with certainty for an infinitely large cluster? From the perspective of simulation, we can't simulate an infinitely large grid, but we can approach this problem by answering the easier question we asked earlier. If a cluster, with probability of 100%, can't percolate through the grid, then an infinite cluster is not possible.

Let's call such a threshold probability p_c where c stands for critical.

An Analytical Solution for the 1-D Case

Although this book is about simulation, I want to show you how the 1-D case is solved analytically.

For either site percolation or bond percolation in 1-D, the critical probability p_c is 1. It is easy to visualize; there is one and only one way to form an infinite cluster in 1-D. Therefore, any probability smaller than 1 will stop the formation of an infinite cluster.

Let's say the probability that a cluster with size L exists is denoted by $P(p, L)$, then the critical probability must satisfy the following equation:

$$\left[\lim_{L\to\infty} P(p,L) = \left\{ \begin{matrix} 0 & p<p_c \\ 1 & p>p_c \end{matrix} \right] \right.$$

Luckily, the exact expression of $P(p, L)$ is easy to derive:

$$\left[\lim_{L\to\infty} P(p,L) = \lim_{L\to\infty} p^L = \left\{ \begin{matrix} 0 & p<1 \\ 1 & p=1 \end{matrix} \right] \right.$$

Therefore, our critical probability p_c is 1.

From 1-D to 2-D, the difficulty of analytical derivation increases dramatically. In fact, it takes about 20 years for mathematicians to obtain/prove the analytical form of critical probability for the 2-D square grid bond percolation case. Harry Kesten proved that the bond percolation critical probability is exactly $\frac{1}{2}$ in the 2-D square grid case. The site percolation case, on the other hand, is notoriously hard to derive. It turns out that we can only run a simulation to estimate it. The approach is something you already saw in Chapter 1.

A Simulation for the 2-D Case

We will perform the simulation in two steps. For the first part, let's write a function to detect whether there is a cluster that percolates the grid and color it in gray. Our goal is to only find one, so once we find one, we will stop exploring other possible clusters.

For the second part, we will run the simulation multiple times to approximate the critical probability p_c.

To discover the existence of a percolating cluster, we need to write a graph traversal algorithm to traverse through the neighboring occupied sites. There are two options: one is breadth-first search, and the other is depth-first search. Here, I implement the depth-first search algorithm. The idea is to recursively visit neighbors until a longest possible path is visited, then hop back to another possible path in the previous round of recursion.

```
def dfs(self, site, visited) -> None:
      visited.add(site) (1)
      (w,h) = site
      neighbors = [site for site in [(w-1,h),(w+1,h),(w,h-1),(w,h+1)] if
    self.filter_illegal_site(site)]
      for neighbor in neighbors:
          if neighbor not in visited and self.states[neighbor[0]]
        [neighbor[1]] == State.Working:
              self.dfs(neighbor, visited)
```

Next, we write another function for the heavy lifting of finding the cluster. We start from the lowest row of the grid and start searching for clusters whenever we encounter an occupied site. If during the search, we find a site that is on the top edge of the grid, our mission is complete. If we find no site on the lower edge that leads to a percolating cluster, then the search finishes as well.

```
def percolate_through(self):
      clusters = []
      success = False
```

```
        for w in range(self.width):
            if clusters:
                all_visited = reduce(lambda x,y: x.union(y), clusters) (1)
            else:
                all_visited = set()
            if self.states[w][0] == State.Working and (w,0) not in all_
            visited:
                clusters.append(set())
                self.dfs((w,0), clusters[-1])

                latest_cluster = clusters[-1]
                if max([site[1] for site in latest_cluster]) == self.
                height-1:
                    success = True
                    return clusters[-1], success
        return None, success

    def filter_illegal_site(self, site): (2)
        (w,h) = site
        if w < 0 or w >= self.width:
            return False
        if h < 0 or h >= self.height:
            return False
        return True
```

We can also update other parts of our program to enable the highlighting of the percolating cluster. Here are the key lines. You can find the complete code in the online site of this book.

```
class State(Enum):
    Working = 1
    Broken = 0
    Cluster = -1

class Grid:
    state_to_color = {State.Broken: "red",
                      State.Working: "blue",
                      State.Cluster: "gray"}
```

```
def render(self, return_array = False, block_size = 1300, percolating
= False):
    if percolating:
        cluster, success = self.percolate_through()
        if success:
            for site in cluster:
                w, h = site
                self.states[w][h] = State.Cluster
```

Note that the method should only run once. The correctness of the depth-first search algorithm guarantees the discovery of one percolating cluster if it does exist.

Alright, let's run a rendering of a simulation to see if we can find a percolating cluster with different grid sizes and occupation probabilities. First, let's try a grid with size of 10 by 10 and occupation probability of 0.5:

```
Grid(width=10, height = 10, random_init= True, prob = 0.5).
render(percolating = True)
```

We are lucky! There is one percolating cluster! The gray sites in Figure 5-3 show the percolating cluster.

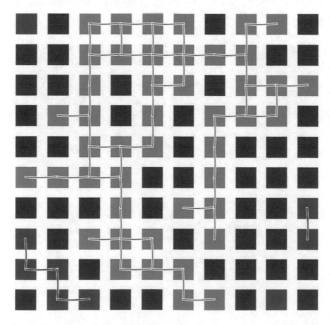

Figure 5-3. *A grid with a percolating cluster*

Let's run the code again; we get another not-so-lucky result as shown in Figure 5-4.

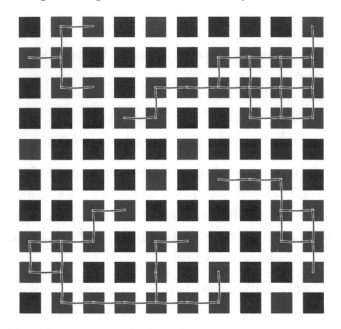

Figure 5-4. *A grid without a percolating cluster*

Let's try a much larger 100 by 100 square grid with occupation probability 0.7. The result is shown in Figure 5-5.

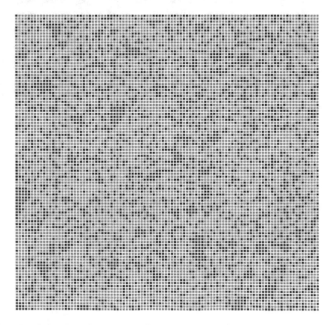

Figure 5-5. *A 100 by 100 grid with a percolating cluster*

I hope your eyes are still working OK. The percolating cluster is so big that it contains almost all the occupied sites. You may also run into the recursion depth error; you can temporarily increase the maximum recursion depth by setting the *sys.setrecursionlimit* parameter.

Next, let's run a simulation to see if we can narrow down the value of the critical occupation probability p_c. First, let's try a grid with size of 10 by 10 and occupation probability ranging from 0.2 to 0.8 with a step of 0.05. Totally, we will have about 13 settings. We will run each setting 100 times to obtain the probability of p_c where L is the size of the grid.

```
L = 10
ROUND = 100
p_clustering = []
for prob in np.linspace(0.2,0.8,num=13):
    res = []
    for _ in range(ROUND):
        _, success = Grid(L, L, prob = prob, random_init = True).percolate_
        through()
        res.append(success)
    p_clustering.append(np.mean(res))

with plt.xkcd():
    fig, ax = plt.subplots(figsize=(10,8))
    ax.plot(x = np.linspace(0.2,0.8,num=13), y = p_clustering, marker="*")
    ax.set_xlabel("Occupation Probability")
    ax.set_ylabel("Probability of Percolation")
    ax.set_title("10 by 10 Grid Percolation Experiment")
```

Our result should agree with our intuition. When the occupation probability is low, we should see no percolating cluster at all. When it is large, the probability of percolation should approach 1. Check Figure 5-6 for the relationship.

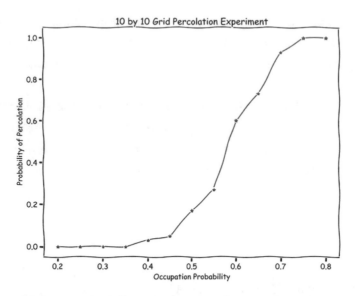

Figure 5-6. *Percolating probability changes with respect to the occupation probability for a 10 by 10 grid*

It looks like somewhere between 0.5 and 0.6, there is a jump of the percolation probability.

Let's enlarge our grid to 50 by 50 and try again. Note that this may take longer time and deeper recursion depth. The result is in Figure 5-7.

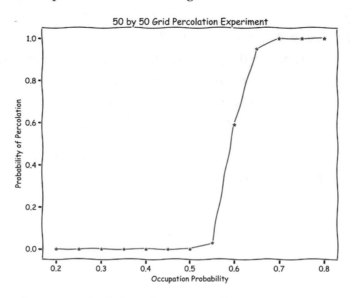

Figure 5-7. *Percolating probability changes with respect to the occupation probability for a 50 by 50 grid*

The trend becomes more obvious. The formation of the percolating cluster becomes almost certain once a threshold around *0.6* is exceeded. Now, let's focus on the range between *0.5* and *0.7* and zoom in. We obtain Figure 5-8.

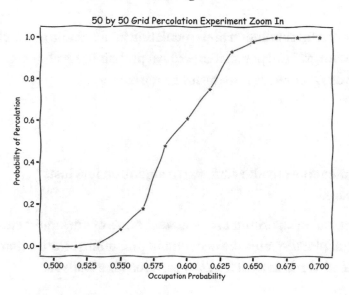

Figure 5-8. *Zoom in for a 50 by 50 grid*

Before moving on to the next section, let's run the simulation for a 100 by 100 grid and 1000 runs for each occupation probability data point. Figure 5-9 is what I got.

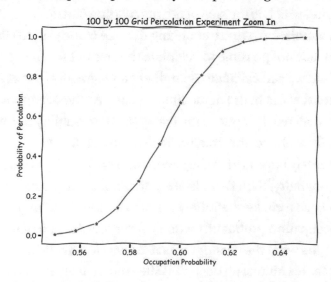

Figure 5-9. *Percolating probability changes with respect to the occupation probability for a 100 by 100 grid*

Note that although the shapes of the curves are similar, the range of the x axis is much smaller: it is also a zoom-in visualization. Our estimation of the critical probability is more and more accurate. We can see clearly that the critical occupation probability is around 0.6.

With more powerful simulation and calculation in academic research, the current estimation of square grid site percolation critical probability is about *0.592746*. We will use this value as our *ground truth* in the following content.

Exercise

1. Implement the breadth-first search algorithm for cluster discovery.

2. Implement an algorithm to calculate the size of the largest cluster of a grid. Plot it against the occupation probability. Notice that you may need to run several times to get a sensible statistic.

Another Interesting Statistic in 2-D Grid Percolation

If we go back to our original forest fire question, a question we are more interested in is the severity of the fire, which is the size of the percolating cluster.

However, as in simulation, we are changing the size of the grid to simulate an infinitely large grid. It is not possible to calculate the size of the largest cluster as it is grid size dependent. What we can calculate is another value, fraction *f*, that is the fraction of the occupied sites that are in the percolating cluster. As the occupation probability grows, the fraction shall reach 1, but as the occupation probability approaches the critical probability from above, the fraction shall approach 0.

Imagine an infinitely large grid, if the occupation probability is just slightly bigger than the critical probability, then there is one percolating cluster. Although probability theory tells us that such a cluster definitely exists in an infinitely large grid, even a slightest smaller occupation probability won't even allow the percolating cluster to form! Can you imagine what the cluster looks like? Yes. It is likely to be very zigzagging, infinitely large but leaves almost all occupied sites out of itself. Sounds contradictory but it is true.

First, let's implement a new method to calculate the fraction:

```
def percolating_cluster_fraction(self):
    assert(self.percolated)
    total_occupied = sum([sum([h in(State.Cluster, State.Working) for h in
    row]) for row in self.states])
    cluster_size = sum([sum([h  == State.Cluster for h in row]) for row in
    self.states])
    return cluster_size/total_occupied
```

Next, we run a simulation to evaluate the relationship between the fraction and the occupation probability. We use a 100 by 100 grid, 200 by 200 grid, and 300 by 300 grid to perform the simulation. From above the ground truth, we slowly decrease the occupation probability to around 0.59, and for each one, we perform 1000 runs to obtain the average.

```
L = 100
ROUND = 1000
TRUTH = 0.592746
fractions = []
probs = []
start = 0.622746
steps = 110
step = (start - TRUTH)/(steps - 10)
for i in tqdm(range(steps)):
    res = []
    prob = start - i * step
    probs.append(prob)
    for _ in range(ROUND):
        while True:
            grid = Grid(L, L, prob = prob, random_init = True)
            grid.percolate_through()
            if grid.percolated:
                frac = grid.percolating_cluster_fraction()
                res.append(frac)
                break
    fractions.append(res)
```

We can then estimate how much the fraction is when the critical occupation probability is reached. The plotting code is trivial and therefore skipped. We obtain Figure 5-10.

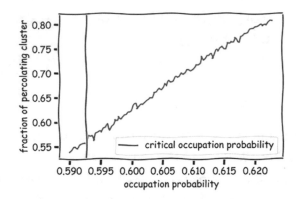

Figure 5-10. *The fraction of a percolating cluster vs. the occupation probability for a 100 by 100 grid*

Well, this doesn't look good because ideally the fraction should be 0; instead, we get a value around *0.57*. Let's try a larger 200 by 200 grid. We obtain Figure 5-11.

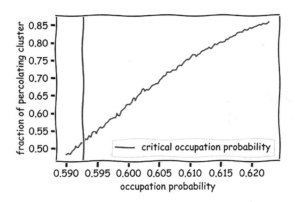

Figure 5-11. *The fraction of a percolating cluster vs. the occupation probability for a 200 by 200 grid*

A 200 by 200 grid size gives us a fraction about *0.52* at critical occupation probability. Note that this simulation runs for hours on my 2019 MacBook Pro, 16GB RAM. If you have a machine that you can leave on for a whole day, you can try the 300 by 300 grid size simulation just as I did. I have to set the max recursion depth to a fairly large number to avoid the recursion error. After hours and hours of calculation, I obtained Figure 5-12.

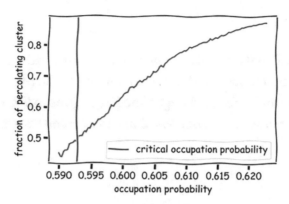

Figure 5-12. *The fraction of a percolating cluster vs. the occupation probability for a 300 by 300 grid*

We successfully reached a fraction value of *0.5* at critical occupation probability, but we are far from the theoretical value. This is an example to demonstrate how difficult it can be to get a simulation's result to converge. The difficulty of simulating around the critical occupation probability is well known because we are approaching a so-called *phase transition* in the simulation. The property of the system changes abruptly around the critical occupation probability. We are using a naive way to perform the simulation, and our hardware is not powerful enough as well. This was expected. Don't feel frustrated.

Exercise

1. Can you derive the analytical equation for the fraction as a function of the occupation probability in the 1-D case?

2. The *percolate_through* method will stop searching for potential percolating clusters when the first one is found. Estimate how likely it is for two non-overlapping percolating clusters to coexist.

3. Perform the bond percolation simulation for a grid of size 100 by 100. Plot the fraction of the percolating cluster as a function of the occupation probability as well.

Summary

In this chapter, we studied the simulation of percolation on grids. This type of simulation has a deep root in mathematics and theoretical physics. We derived an analytical solution for a 1-D case and simulated larger and larger grids in 2-D cases. We also saw one *painful* example that sometimes simulation can become extremely hard.

## CHAPTER 6

Queuing System: How Stock Trades Are Made

A stock exchange is a fascinating system in which people trade stocks and wish to profit from the trading. In the old times before electronic trading, brokers would get together and trade stocks on behalf of their clients by yelling at each other. Nowadays, everything becomes electronic. The retailer investors can use mobile applications or web applications to make trades.

In this chapter, we will build a system to simulate a stock exchange and visualize an order book. The key takeaway for this simulation is the handling of the queuing of orders. For example, some orders are submitted early, while others are submitted late with a lower price. We need to properly determine the order priority in such cases. On the other hand, we also need to manage the message broadcasting. In real life, investors can see the real-time stock price changes which are broadcasted by the stock exchange.

Trading Process Fundamentals

First, let's decompose the trading process to identify what entities and processes should be simulated.

There are three major parts in a successful trade. First, the investor sends an order to the exchange. Then, a *match engine* receives the order and tries to find the counterpart of the order. For example, if a new sell order comes in, the *match engine* will try to find an existing buy order in the queued orders to match the new sell order. In the following third step, there are two possibilities. If there is a successful find, the trade will be completed, and messages of successful trade will be broadcasted to the original investors, and a new price will also be available, as the latest price may change due to the trade, to all investors in the market. If there is no successful find, the new sell order will also be queued until future trades come in. Investors can also request removal of their queued orders.

© Rongpeng Li and Aiichiro Nakano 2022
R. Li and A. Nakano, *Simulation with Python*, https://doi.org/10.1007/978-1-4842-8185-7_6

In a short summary, we need to simulate the following entities:

1. Investor

2. Match engine

Well, it also makes sense to further split the match engine to more components like one part is solely responsible for match trades and another part is responsible for broadcasting information, etc. However, for simplicity, we will pack everything on the stock market side into the match engine entity.

To fully simulate the trading process, the following four processes need to be simulated:

1. The investor sends an order to the match engine.

2. The match engine processes and tries to match the trade.

3. The match engine broadcasts messages to the original order submitters if there is a successful trade.

4. The match engine broadcasts the latest prices to *everyone* in the market.

Due to the limitation of space, our focus for this chapter is on the first two parts. However, you can tell that steps 3 and 4 are just the opposites of step 1. I will leave these two parts as exercises to you at the end of the book. You will see that there are many simplifications and assumptions in this chapter. I will leave all of them as exercises for you to implement a fully functional system.

The Order Book

The way the match engine keeps track of orders is to maintain an *order book*. An order book is a dynamic list of buy and sell orders that keeps getting updated by the match engine. You can visualize the order book as two piles of orders; all the buy orders are on the left, while the sell orders are on the right. The match engine tries to find tradable pairs from the buying side and the selling side.

The order book needs to be maintained such that all participants in the market feel fair and equal. There are certain principles that need to be respected. There are two most important ones.

First, sell orders with a lower price have priority over sell orders with a higher price. By the same token, buy orders with a higher price have priority over buy orders with a lower price. However, this is only true for the so-called *limit order*. The *market order* is special because it will accept any prices. For example, a market buy order will match the sell orders from the lowest price to higher price until the requested amount of shares in the buy order has been all filled, which may significantly push the *market price*, the price every participant sees, higher.

On the other hand, there are *stop loss* orders and *stop profit* orders. Such orders will be triggered when the price hits a certain level. For example, a stop loss order will be executed once the price drops to a certain level to control the loss. We won't cover such types of orders in this chapter, but readers are encouraged to implement them as extensions of our simulation.

Second, if the prices are the same, orders that were submitted earlier have higher priority. Note that in principle there won't be two orders with the exact same submitting time so there will always be an order to rely on.

As orders come in, the order book will dynamically change; the volume of orders at a certain price level is called the *depth*. The deeper the depth is, the more interest there is for buying or selling the stocks. As we discussed earlier, the orders with a price closer to the *market price* will have higher priority than the orders further away from it. Therefore, the order book will always look like a *valley* with fast changing depths. GIF 6-1 illustrates it clearly.

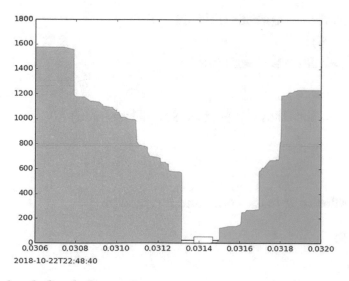

GIF 6-1. Order book depth dynamics

Note that in real life, if an order hasn't been executed by the match engine, the investors can always request to cancel the order. However, we won't implement this part either in this chapter. You can give it a try; it is not as hard as you may think.

Create the Interfaces and Determine the Data Schema

Alright! We are ready to build a match engine now. First, let's create an *endpoint* that can accept orders. To do that, we are going to use *flask* to build a simple API (application programming interface). An API exposes certain functionality to external users and other programs. In our case, our API does one thing: accept the incoming order.

If you haven't tried flask earlier, here is an example to get you started.

Let's install the two libraries we are going to use first:

```
pip3 install flask, requests
```

Next, create an *engine.py* file with your favorite editor; copy and paste the following code:

```
from flask import Flask

app = Flask(__name__)

@app.route('/submit',  methods = ['GET'])
def process_order():
    return '<h1>order received</h1>'

def main():
    app.run(host='localhost', port=8080, debug=True)

if __name__ == '__main__':
    main()
```

Now, run this flask *app* in the command line by typing

```
python engine.py
```

You should see the following messages. Note that your exact *debugger PIN* may be different from mine.

```
* Serving Flask app 'app' (lazy loading)
 * Environment: production
   WARNING: This is a development server. Do not use it in a production
   deployment.
   Use a production WSGI server instead.
 * Debug mode: on
 * Running on http://localhost:8080/ (Press CTRL+C to quit)
 * Restarting with stat
 * Debugger is active!
 * Debugger PIN: 374-303-372
```

We just created the simplest web app! If you open your browser and navigate to `http://localhost:8080/submit`, you will see a message as in Figure 6-1.

order received

Figure 6-1. *Order received message from the website*

Very cool!

With less than ten lines, we created an endpoint, with the *process_order* function, that users can visit and interact with our application. Our application does only one thing: it returns some *bytes* that a browser will interpret as a string with level 1 heading. That's why you see such a large font.

Notice that the *process_order* function has a parameter *method*, the desired method is *GET*. This regulates which method this */submit* endpoint accepts. The GET method allows users to *get* stuff from this endpoint only. If users try to send something to this endpoint, the request will fail as it is not allowed, for now.

Our simulated investors, which I often refer to as *bots*, can't refresh browsers to interact with our stock exchange. Let's see whether we can use Python to do it. Now, in another file called *bot.py*, copy and paste the following code snippet. Run it while keeping the *engine.py* running in the previous terminal.

```python
import requests
from time import sleep

for i in range(10):
    res = requests.get('http://localhost:8080/submit')
    print(res.content.decode('utf-8'))
    sleep(1)
```

Here, we use the *requests* library to get information from the engine.py application for ten times with a break of one second between two consecutive requests.

The URL in the code has three parts. The *http* is the protocol name which stands for hypertext transfer protocol. Similarly, there are *https* or *ftp* protocols for a secure version of http and file transfer. The *localhost* is the *hostname* (also called *domain name*), while *8080* is the *port number*. Together the hostname and the port number define *where* the application is. Both the hostname and the port number are specified in the *engine.py* file when we start the application. The path */submit* is specified in the *process_order* function as well; it is often called *path to resources*. Users can visit this path to retrieve certain information which is treated as a kind of *resource*.

Now, let's transform the elementary example to real useful code for our match engine simulation. The match engine should be able to accept *payload* from investors (bots) that contain order information. However, we need to figure out what information should go into that payload first from the investor side.

From the perspective of the investor, at a minimum, the payload should have the type of the order (whether it is a market order or a limit order), the size of the order (how many shares the investor plans to buy/sell), and the direction of the order (whether it is a buy order or a sell order). If the order is a limit order, a price should also be specified.

From the perspective of the stock exchange, a timestamp and an ID are also required. The timestamp is needed to determine the priority of equal-price limit orders. The ID is used to identify the order so corresponding actions can be taken when the order is canceled or executed.

In general, an ID for an entity is always required. For simplicity, we will allow the investor/bot to set the ID and send the payload to the match engine. The ID will be created from the id() method plus randomization, so it is unlikely that there will be any collision in our simulation. Also note that sometimes an order can be filled partially. We will implement the partial fulfillment feature.

In summary, the payload from the investor should look like the following:

```
from flask import Flask
from flask import request, jsonify
import json
import time

app = Flask(__name__)

@app.route('/submit',  methods = ['POST'])
def process_order():
    order = request.get_json(force=True)
    order["submit_timestamp"] = time.time()
    print(order) # for testing purpose
    return jsonify({"status": "received"})

def main():
    app.run(host='localhost', port=8080, debug=True)

if __name__ == '__main__':
    main()
```

Note that we import the *request* and *jsonify* modules to process the posted data and send back an acknowledgment to the bot.

To accommodate such change, our *bot.py* has one more function to generate fake orders. It looks like the following now:

```
import requests
from time import sleep
import random
import json

def generate_order():
    return {
        "order_id": id(random.random()),
        "order_type":random.choice(["market", "limit"]),
        "order_size": random.randint(1, 100),
        "order_price": random.randint(1, 100), # will be ignored if the order
        type is market
```

```
        "order_direction": random.choice(["buy", "sell"]),
    }

for i in range(10):
    order = generate_order()
    res = requests.post('http://localhost:8080/submit',
                        data = json.dumps(order))
    print(res.json())
    sleep(1)
```

Implement Order Book Logic

The next step is to implement a proper data structure to maintain the order book. We will use a dictionary of lists to maintain each side of the orders. For example, on the buy side, we will use a dictionary of lists to keep track of all the orders.

The dictionary keys are the order prices. The price of a stock is not infinitely accurate, which means there is a minimal step. For example, it is either 1.5 dollar per share or 1.6 dollar per share, but not 1.55 dollar per share. This ensures that there are always a manageable number of keys in the dictionary, so sorting the keys is fairly straightforward.

Each value in the dictionary is a list of the submitted orders. The list behaves like a queue, without allowing order cancellation, so that earlier orders get matched early if there is a suitable counterpart in the market.

Let's check the code for the *OrderBook* class and corresponding order receiving code:

```
from collections import defaultdict
import numpy

class OrderBook:
    def __init__(self):
        self.buy_orders = defaultdict(list)
        self.sell_orders = defaultdict(list)
        self.latest_ordr = None

    def receive_orders(self, order):
        if order["order_type"] == "market":
```

```
        order["order_price"] = np.inf if order["order_direction"] ==
        "buy" else -np.inf
            # willing to buy at extreme high price
    if order["order_direction"] == "buy":
        self.buy_orders[order["order_price"]].append(order)
    else:
        self.sell_orders[order["order_price"]].append(order)

    self.latest_order = order
    self.fulfill_orders()

def fulfill_orders(self):
    raise NotImplementedError
```

Can you tell how I implemented market orders? If a buy order is a market order, then I set the accepted price to positive infinity. It means that the buy order will accept an arbitrarily high price. The same applies to the market sell orders which will accept arbitrarily low prices to sell. Once the price is determined, we simply find the list, as the value of the dictionary, and append our new order to it. This is where *defaultdict* makes the code cleaner: if the list doesn't exist yet, *defaultdict* will create an empty list for us.

Note that we have an unimplemented function called *fulfill_orders*. It is responsible for actually fulfilling the order, and it is the key in this code. Let's check it out:

```
def fulfill_orders(self):
        """

        # When this method runs, there should be only one of the
        following three cases possible.
        1. There is one and only one market order that can be executed
           with the tip of the opposite side
        2. There is no market order
            2.1 There is no matching opposite orders
            2.2 The latest limited order can be executed by fulfilling
                the orders on the opposite side one by one

        The three cases are mutually exclusive so we will handle that
        one by one.
        """
```

```python
latest_order = self.latest_order.copy()

opposite_orderbook = self.buy_orders if latest_order[
    "order_direction"] == "sell" else self.sell_orders

if latest_order["order_direction"] == "buy":
    opposite_prices = sorted(opposite_orderbook.keys())
else:
    opposite_prices = sorted(opposite_orderbook.keys(),
    reverse=True)

for opposite_price in opposite_prices:

    valid_buy = latest_order["order_direction"] == "buy" and
    opposite_price <= latest_order["order_price"]

    valid_sell = latest_order["order_direction"] == "sell" and
    opposite_price >= latest_order["order_price"]

    valid = (valid_buy or valid_sell) and latest_order["order_
    size"] > 0

    if not valid:
        break

    for queued_order in opposite_orderbook[opposite_price]:
        if queued_order["order_size"] <= latest_
        order["order_size"]:
            latest_order["order_size"] -= queued_
            order["order_size"]

            if latest_order["order_direction"] == "buy":
                self.buy_orders[latest_order["order_
                price"]][-1]["order_size"] -= queued_
                order["order_size"]
            else:
                self.sell_orders[latest_order["order_
                price"]][-1]["order_size"] -= queued_
                order["order_size"]
```

```
        fill_size = queued_order["order_size"]
        queued_order["order_size"] = 0

    elif latest_order["order_size"] > 0:
        # print("the latest order is not big enough to eat
        the current queued order")
        queued_order["order_size"] -= latest_
        order["order_size"]

        fill_size = latest_order["order_size"]
        # mark the latest_order completely fulfilled.
        latest_order["order_size"] = 0
        # the latest order will always be the last one. Set
        its size to 0 since it is depleted now.
        if latest_order["order_direction"] == "buy":
            self.buy_orders[latest_order["order_price"]]
            [-1]["order_size"] = 0
        else:
            self.sell_roders[latest_order["order_price"]]
            [-1]["order_size"] = 0

    else:
        break
self.clean_limit_orderbook()
```

Note that certain lines of the code are quite long, but the inline comments should be sufficient for you to understand. Basically, there are three steps:

1. First, determine the direction of the latest order because our order book will and only will be changed by the latest order.

2. Once the direction is determined, check whether there is a possible trade. If the latest order is a market order, then we don't need to check the prices of the opposite side orders; otherwise, we need to make sure that there is an overlap. For example, if the latest order is a buy order, then the lowest sell order price should be no higher than the latest buy order.

3. Then we iterate eligible opposite orders in the order of submission time, from earliest to latest to enforce fairness, until the latest order's volume is depleted. There is another chance that there are no more opposite orders, in the condition that there is a huge market order, but that is very unlikely.

Following the logic, the code should be fairly easy to read.

For cleanness, we can also implement a *clean_limit_orderbook* function to run after the order fulfillment. This may not be necessary, but it is helpful for utility helper functions like *print_orderbook* which is defined as follows:

```
def print_orderbook(self):
    print("-------------------Orderbook-------------------")
    for price in sorted(self.sell_orders.keys(), reverse= True):
        depth = sum(map(lambda order: order["order_size"], self.sell_
        orders[price]))
        print("sell side price: {}, depth: {}".format(price, depth))
    print("-----------------------------------------------")
    for price in sorted(self.buy_orders.keys(),reverse= True):
        depth = sum(map(lambda order: order["order_size"], self.buy_
        orders[price]))
        print("buy side price: {}, depth: {}".format(price, depth))
    print("\n")
```

Lastly, here is the implementation of the *clean_limit_orderbook* function, fairly straightforward:

```
def clean_limit_orderbook(self):
    """
    Remove useless keys in the limit order book
    """
    for orderbook in [self.buy_orders, self.sell_orders]:
        empty_prices = []
        for price in orderbook.keys():
            new_orders = list(filter(lambda order: order["order_size"]
            > 0, orderbook[price]))
```

```
        if len(new_orders) == 0:
            empty_prices.append(price)
        else:
            orderbook[price] = new_orders

    for price in empty_prices:
        del orderbook[price]
```

Hook the Bots and Engine Together

Hooking the bot and the engine together is straightforward now. Let's modify our *engine. py* file to process the order and build the order book:

```
from orderbook import OrderBook

orderbook = OrderBook()

app = Flask(__name__)

@app.route('/submit',  methods = ['POST'])
def process_order():
    order = request.get_json(force=True)
    order["submit_timestamp"] = time.time()
    orderbook.receive_orders(order)
    return jsonify({"status": "received"})
```

To get a sensible order book structure, we also need to change the order type frequencies. If there are too many market orders, then the order book will be depleted very quickly without showing a valley structure. So let's change one line in the *generate_ order* function in the *bot.py* file:

```
"order_type":random.choice(["market", "limit","limit","limit","limit",
"limit","limit","limit","limit","limit"]),
```

So, basically, we are stating that nine out of ten times, the order will be a limit order.

With this setting, we can submit 1000 orders and print out the order book at the end of simulation by calling the *print_orderbook* method; you will see something like the following:

```
------------------Orderbook-------------------
sell side price: 100, depth: 816
sell side price: 99, depth: 1511
sell side price: 98, depth: 1325
sell side price: 97, depth: 1063
sell side price: 96, depth: 1262
sell side price: 95, depth: 1314
sell side price: 94, depth: 1227
sell side price: 93, depth: 1350
sell side price: 92, depth: 1392
sell side price: 91, depth: 1105
sell side price: 90, depth: 722
sell side price: 89, depth: 1260
sell side price: 88, depth: 716
sell side price: 87, depth: 922
sell side price: 86, depth: 809
sell side price: 85, depth: 1040
sell side price: 84, depth: 1066
sell side price: 83, depth: 1038
sell side price: 82, depth: 943
sell side price: 81, depth: 1312
sell side price: 80, depth: 605
sell side price: 69, depth: 12
sell side price: 64, depth: 23
sell side price: 63, depth: 39
sell side price: 43, depth: 84
sell side price: 31, depth: 80
------------------------------------------------
buy side price: 30, depth: 55
buy side price: 28, depth: 67
buy side price: 22, depth: 72
buy side price: 21, depth: 189
buy side price: 20, depth: 63
buy side price: 19, depth: 71
buy side price: 18, depth: 154
```

```
buy side price: 16, depth: 213
buy side price: 15, depth: 390
buy side price: 14, depth: 413
buy side price: 13, depth: 649
buy side price: 12, depth: 841
buy side price: 11, depth: 900
buy side price: 10, depth: 1068
buy side price: 9, depth: 982
buy side price: 8, depth: 1477
buy side price: 7, depth: 748
buy side price: 6, depth: 1271
buy side price: 5, depth: 1704
buy side price: 4, depth: 1514
buy side price: 3, depth: 1511
buy side price: 2, depth: 956
buy side price: 1, depth: 1102
```

It is quite clear that the depths around the current market price are smaller. The visualizations are left to you as an exercise. See the following section for details.

Exercises and Extension Ideas

In this section, I will lay out five ideas that can significantly extend the functionalities of our stock exchange. They are ordered according to their levels of difficulty.

Multiple Bots

In our simulation, we only use one bot so basically we are trading with ourselves, which makes no sense. You can extend the order's data schema to allow a new field called *bot_id* or *investor_id* such that only different bots can trade with each other.

Note that the bots' IDs need to be a limited set. You can simulate arbitrage cases, which means a bot can submit a buy order and a sell order at the same time to profit from the price volatility.

An Informed Bot

An intelligent investor will not trade blindly. They need to know what the current *market price* is in order to make a wise decision. The match engine can send the latest price to an external *monitor* so every bot can check it.

Order Book Visualization

The *print_orderbook* method is not good enough. Let's replace it with a new *visualize_orderbook* method. Can you make an animation out of it?

Order Cancellation Support

Let's support the order cancellation functionality. If a bot requests to cancel an order, maybe through a different *resource path* called */cancel*, the match engine should be able to locate the order quickly and kick it out of the queue for that price. Can you think of a way to do this efficiently?

Stop Orders Support

Since order cancellation is supported, why not take one step further to support the stop orders? If a bot submits a stop loss order, the match engine should only execute the order when the price hits the stop loss line. Do your own research and implement this feature efficiently and fairly to all market participants.

Summary

In this chapter, we studied a queue system. A simulation like this is not only technical but also social. The match engine should operate based on a set of rules to enforce fairness.

## CHAPTER 7

Rock, Scissors, and Paper: Multi-agent Simulation

We have touched so many different kinds of simulations so far. There is another very important type called agent-based simulation (ABS). Sometimes, it is also referred to as agent-based modeling (ABM). Agent-based simulation is an umbrella term that you can categorize a lot of context-specific or domain-specific simulations as agent-based simulation.

What these simulations have in common is that they all simulate the actions and most importantly interactions between so-called autonomous agents and the environment. An agent is just a minimal unit that can take actions. An environment is the collection of external factors, including other agents. For example, our simulation of the stock exchange in Chapter 6 can be treated as an agent-based simulation if you implemented the first extension: adding more than one bot. Different bots interact with each other according to the rules set by the match engine. We focused on the implementation of the rules though.

Agent-based simulation is especially important to understand *emerging behavior*, which means nontrivial phenomena can emerge from trivial rules that govern the actions of agents. For example, the formation of large protein molecules from amino acids is still a mystery although the single amino acid seems pretty simple. In the financial market, different investors behave to maximize their own interest. The intention seems straightforward, but collectively the actions may lead to unexpected crashes.

Now let's dive into it.

© Rongpeng Li and Aiichiro Nakano 2022
R. Li and A. Nakano, *Simulation with Python*, https://doi.org/10.1007/978-1-4842-8185-7_7

Community Formation on a Street

First, let's build a simplest agent-based simulation from scratch: the Schelling model of segregation. This is a model by economist Thomas Schelling. The idea is simple; without external factors, people in a region will move or stay in their original spots according to their similarities with their neighborhoods. Ultimately, different communities will form spontaneously.

You may recognize that the idea has common characteristics as the forest fire percolation model we discussed in an earlier chapter. That's right. They are both on a *grid* with *agents* or *nodes* as elements to change state. However, different from the forest fire one in which a predefined probability controls the behavior of a node, people make decisions to move or stay dynamically as the environment changes in Schelling's model.

For simplicity, we study the Schelling model on a one-dimensional *street* rather than a two-dimensional *community*. The plain English description of the question is the following: suppose there is a street with *N* rental properties; some of them are occupied, and some are open to move in. Let's make an assumption that there is no cost to change properties. There are two kinds of people, *A* and *B*. Both kinds of people love to stay with their own kind. If both their neighbors are of different kinds, they will pick an unoccupied property and move there until the majority of people are happy with their neighbors.

Let's use a *list* data structure to model the street and use *0* to indicate that a spot/rental property is not occupied. We will use *-1* and *1* to indicate a property that is occupied by group *A* or group *B* people. Note this choice is for visualization simplicity as we can easily check the formation of clusters by a scatter plot.

The first version looks straightforward:

```
N = 300
OCCUPATE_RATE = 0.9 # 90% are occupied originally
AB_RATIO = 1 # RATIO of A to B
ROUNDS = 100

street = np.array([0 for _ in range(N)])
for idx, house in enumerate(street):
    if np.random.rand() < OCCUPATE_RATE:
        street[idx] = -1 if np.random.rand() < AB_RATIO/(1+AB_RATIO) else 1

# run simulation until no moves or exceeding maximal round
stable = False
```

```
iteration = 0

while not stable and iteration < ROUNDS:
    print("starting round {}".format(iteration))
    moves = 0
    # obtain the empty properties
    empties = set(i for i, house in enumerate(street) if house == 0)
    for idx, house in enumerate(street):
        if idx > 0 and idx < len(street)-1:
            if street[idx-1]*street[idx] == -1 and
            street[idx+1]*street[idx] == -1:
                # move to a random site
                target = np.random.choice(tuple(empties))
                empties.remove(target)
                empties.add(idx)
                street[target] = street[idx]
                street[idx] = 0
                moves += 1
    if moves == 0:
        break
    iteration += 1
```

Note that several parameters can be adjusted. Our tenants are living on a pretty dense street as 90% of the properties are occupied. Let's take a look at what the street looks like before the simulation starts in Figure 7-1.

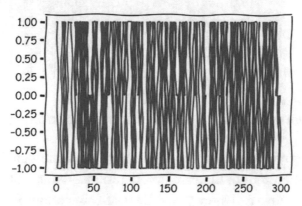

Figure 7-1. *Random occupation pattern before simulation*

113

The strong zigzagging shows that groups A and B are living in an interleaving pattern. Run the iteration, and after four rounds, the system reaches a stable status as shown in Figure 7-2.

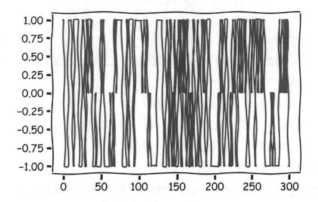

Figure 7-2. *Stable occupation pattern after four rounds of iteration*

As you can see, there are *street segments* which contain only groups A and B.

What if we increase the density to even higher like 98% occupation rate? As the street becomes more crowded, tenants can easily get unhappy, and the clustering can become more prominent.

Here is a randomly generated street with 98% occupation rate as shown in Figure 7-3.

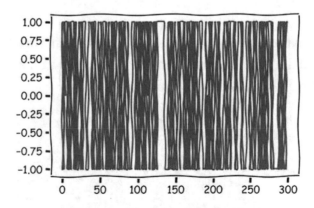

Figure 7-3. *Random occupation pattern with a 98% occupation rate*

Guess what? The enforced 100 times of iterations is not enough. The street remains changing after even hundreds of thousands of iterations. Tenants dislike each other, but they have nowhere to move to. Figure 7-4 is the result after about 100K iterations.

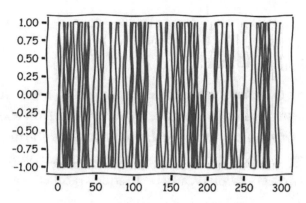

Figure 7-4. *A nonstable occupation pattern with a 98% occupation rate*

Let's try another scenario. Let's say people are unhappy if *one* of their neighbors is of different kinds, rather than *two* of them. How would the simulation change? Intuitively, we should see a more segregated street. If we start with a 90% occupied street, a stable result looks like Figure 7-5.

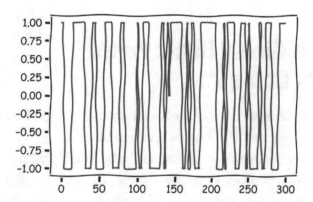

Figure 7-5. *A stable occupation pattern for the one-neighbor-unhappy case*

It is visually clear that larger homogeneous neighborhoods appear. This *emergence* is typical in agent-based simulation. Each agent behaves independently following simple rules that only involve the *local* environment. However, a *global* pattern will emerge nonetheless.

Exercise

Original Schelling Model

In this exercise, please extend our one-dimensional street to a two-dimensional community. This is also closer to Schelling's original model. Now each property has eight neighbors, and we have one more parameter to choose: the number of different numbers that will trigger a relocation. Run your simulation and find such a parameter that triggers significant segregation on a 10 by 10 square grid with an occupation rate of 80%.

Three Groups

In both the one-dimensional case and the two-dimensional case, introduce a third population and run the simulation again. What do you anticipate? Will segregation be more significant or less?

How to Win a Global Rock, Paper, and Scissors Contest

There are many mature libraries for agent-based simulation/modeling. For Python, the most popular and actively maintained one is called Mesa.

Mesa provides a set of core components and scheduling policies for agent-based simulation. This makes fast prototyping and developing possible. For example, we can have an *agent* class and an *environment* class we can inherit from. Each agent can also be *activated* according to different policies. For example, in our Schelling model, we activate agents one by one, which is the so-called *sequential activation*.

Is it possible to allow the tenants on a street to make decisions at the same time? The answer is yes, but the implementation will be trickier. We need to pre-identify all current empty properties and going-to-be empty properties and assign the moving tenants to them simultaneously.

In this example, let's use Mesa to model a contest. Sixteen rock-paper-scissors masters get together and compete with each other. They are arranged into a 4 by 4 grid, and in each round, their choices will be compared with their immediate neighbors (not including diagonal ones). If they are on the winner's side, then they get 1 point for that round; if they lose, –1; if there is a deadlock, then everybody gets a 0.

Well, is it fair for those at the boundary or corner? Naively, it isn't because they have fewer neighbors. However, we can introduce the periodic boundary condition (PBC) to make it fair. Figure 7-6 is an example of the periodic boundary condition in molecular dynamics, in which a molecular has mirrors of itself in fictitious neighboring boxes.

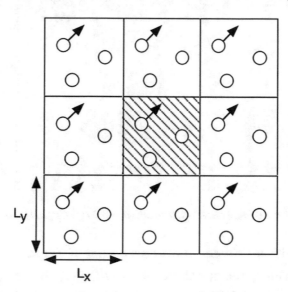

Figure 7-6. *Periodic boundary condition in molecular dynamics*

The periodic boundary condition is ubiquitous in molecular dynamics simulation. The image in Figure 7-6 is taken from Prof. Nakano's lecture slide. The basic idea is to create *replicas* by shifting the system to make the system virtually infinite.

In our contest grid case, if indexed from 0, a contestant at the top-right corner with position (0, 3) will have two normal neighbors at (0,2) and (1,3). But it will also have two *image* neighbors with position (0,0) and (3,3). The idea is illustrated in the visualization in Figure 7-7.

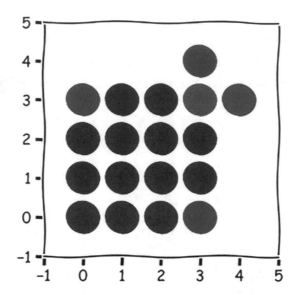

Figure 7-7. The yellow contestant plays with virtual opponents green and blue

The yellow dot indicates a contestant at the corner of the grid, while its *imaginary* blue up neighbor is actually the one at the bottom right and its *imaginary* green right neighbor is the one at the top left. The corner contestant still has four neighbors, with two being imaginary. The boundary ones will also have four neighbors, with one being imaginary. The contest's fairness is restored.

The contestants are separated into two kinds of strategists: one group is stubborn who will likely stick to a choice with a high probability and occasionally change with lower probability, then stick to the new one with high probability. For example, if one starts with paper, then the contestant sticks to paper with a probability of 80% for the following round, then occasionally changes to scissors or rock with a probability of 10%, respectively. Once changed, the contestant sticks to the new one with high probability. They don't care about the result of the current round at all. We call this group *the stubborn* contestants.

Another group is trying to be smart by playing a psychology game. They always pick the move that counters the last round's winning move. For example, if in the last round, rock wins, then they will pick paper for the current round because paper defeats rock. If there is no winner in the last round, then they will randomly pick one. Their idea is that the winner of the round will try to win again with the same move; they can make use of it. We call this group *the sneaky* contestants.

As you can see, both strategies are quite naive. The question now is that if there are eight stubborn contestants and eight sneaky ones arranged in an interleaving pattern on the grid, which group will have a higher average score if they play the game for 100 rounds?

First, let's see how Mesa codes are organized in general:

```python
from mesa import Model, Agent
from mesa.time import SimultaneousActivation

class NewAgent(Agent):

    def __init__(self):
        pass

    def step(self):
        pass

class NewModel(Model):

    def __init__(self):
        self.schedule = SimultaneousActivation(self)
        pass

    def step(self):
        pass
```

From the Mesa library, we import two classes to inherit: *Model* and *Agent*. An agent has a *step* method which defines how agents behave in each round of simulation. A model class also has a *step* method, which defines how the model as a whole evolves in a step.

A model also has a schedule instance. In this case, it is called *SimultaneousActivation*. There are also random activation, sequential activation, etc. The *SimultaneousActivation* policy means all agents will act simultaneously which is necessary for our contest simulation to be *fair*.

Here is our actual code. Let's look at some helper classes first:

```
from enum import Enum

class Type(Enum):
    STUBBORN = 1
    SNEAKY = 0

class Move(Enum):
    Scissors = 0
    Rock = 1
    Paper = -1

    def __lt__(self, other):
        if self == Move.Scissors and other == Move.Rock:
            return True
        if self == Move.Rock and other == Move.Paper:
            return True
        if self == Move.Paper and other == Move.Scissors:
            return True
        return False
```

We define two enumerations for the agent types and the moves they pick. In the *Move* class, we defined a *__lt__* special method to control how two Move instances should be compared. __lt__ stands for *less than*. The method returns True if the instance on the left side of the comparison is smaller than the right side one.

```
Move.Scissors < Move.Rock == True
Move.Rock == Move.Paper == False
```

Now, let's take a look at our code for *Agent*:

```
from mesa import Model, Agent
from mesa.time import SimultaneousActivation
from mesa.space import SingleGrid
from mesa.datacollection import DataCollector
import random

class GameAgent(Agent):
```

```python
def __init__(self, unique_id, pos, model, contestant_type):
    super().__init__(pos, model)
    self.unique_id = unique_id
    self.pos = pos
    self.contestant_type = contestant_type
    self.scores = []
    self.score = 0
    self.move = random.choice(list(Move))

def step(self):

    self.score = 0
    # find all neighbors
    neighbors = [neighbor for neighbor in self.model.grid.neighbor_
    iter(self.pos)]
    neighbor_moves = [neighbor.move for neighbor in neighbors]
    self.score, winning_move = GameAgent.calculate_score(self.move,
    neighbor_moves)
    # determine next move based on current score
    if self.contestant_type == Type.STUBBORN:
        r = random.random()
        if r < 0.8:
            self.next_move = self.move
        else:
            moves = list(Move)
            moves.remove(self.move)
            self.next_move = random.choice(moves)
    else:
        # sneaky strategy
        if winning_move:
            for move in list(Move):
                if move > winning_move:
                    self.next_move = move
                    break
        else:
            self.next_move = random.choice(list(Move))
```

```
def advance(self):
    self.scores.append(self.score)
    self.move = self.next_move

@staticmethod
def calculate_score(move, all_moves):
    # also return winning move

    if len(set(all_moves + [move])) == 3 or len(set(all_moves +
    [move])) == 1:
        # no winning move, it's a draw
        return 0, None

    win = all(move > other_move or move == other_move for other_move in
    all_moves)
    lose = all(move < other_move or move == other_move for other_move
    in all_moves)
    if win:
        return 1, move
    elif lose:
        return -1, random.choice(all_moves)
    return 0, None
```

An agent is initialized with four parameters. The *model* parameter is the model that contains this agent. This is important because not only the model needs to access data about an agent, an agent also needs to access the model data. This allows an agent to *see* the environment around it. For example, an agent needs to identify its neighbors.

An agent's move is randomly initialized. However, depending on the type of the agent, in each round, the agent will choose the *stubborn* strategy or the *sneaky* strategy. The details are implemented in the *step* method. However, the *next_move* is only calculated in the *step* method but not assigned. The assignment is done in the *advance* method. This method is required if the model's activation policy is *SimultaneousActivation*, as we will see very soon. All agents will update their status simultaneously which guarantees fairness.

The *calculate_score* method is a static method. It functions independent of the agent class, but it is logically associated with it, so we make the method *static*. It calculates the score of a round and the winning move for that round. If there is a draw, the winning move is just *None*.

Now, let's take a look at the model class:

```python
class Contest(Model):

    def __init__(self, height=4, width=4, total_rounds = 100):
        self.height = height
        self.width = width
        self.total_rounds = total_rounds
        self.round = 0

        self.schedule = SimultaneousActivation(self)
        self.grid = SingleGrid(width, height, torus=True)

        self.datacollector = DataCollector(
            model_reporters={"stubborn_avg_score": lambda self: np.mean([np.
            mean(agent.scores) for agent in self.schedule.agents if agent.
            contestant_type == Type.STUBBORN]), "sneaky_avg_score": lambda
            self: np.mean([np.mean(agent.scores) for agent in self.schedule.
            agents if agent.contestant_type == Type.SNEAKY])},)

        for idx, cell in enumerate(self.grid.coord_iter()):
            x = cell[1]
            y = cell[2]
            if (x+y)%2 == 0:
                agent = GameAgent(idx, (x,y), self, Type.STUBBORN)
            else:
                agent = GameAgent(idx, (x, y), self, Type.SNEAKY)
            self.grid.position_agent(agent, (x, y))
            self.schedule.add(agent)

        self.running = True

    def step(self):
        self.schedule.step()
        # collect data
        self.round += 1
        if self.round == self.total_rounds:
            self.running = False
        self.datacollector.collect(self)
```

Our model instance will be initialized with a grid. The grid has a parameter *torus* set to true, which means the periodic boundary condition is applied. The model class also has a data collector attribute to collect data about the model as the simulation proceeds. Here, we collect the average score for the two kinds of agents after each round. These two data collectors are called *model_reporters* whose names are *stubborn_avg_score* and *sneaky_avg_score*. You can also define *agent_reporters* to collect data about agents.

The data collection happens in the *step* method after each round of the simulation.

The initialization of the model also puts agents to the grid cells in an alternative fashion. Note that the agents are not added to the model directly but the *schedule* attribute we discussed earlier: the simultaneous activation policy.

Now, we can run the simulation for 100 rounds:

```
model = Contest(4, 4, 100)

while model.running:
    model.step()
```

The model's data collector collects the global averages. After the run finishes, the data collector can output the result as a pandas dataframe:

```
model.datacollector.get_model_vars_dataframe()
```

You should see something like the following:

```
    stubborn_avg_score      sneaky_avg_score

0        -0.125000          0.000000
1        -0.062500          0.000000
2        -0.083333          0.000000
3        -0.062500          0.031250
4        -0.050000          0.025000
...         ...                ...
95       -0.011719          0.013021
96       -0.011598          0.011598
97       -0.011480          0.010204
98       -0.012626          0.011364
99       -0.016250          0.013750

100 rows × 2 columns
```

The longer we run, the more data an agent's *scores* list accumulates. It looks like in this round, a *sneaky* strategy is slightly better. Is it convincing?

Run it again; I get the following:

```
stubborn_avg_score    sneaky_avg_score

0        0.000000      0.000000
1        0.000000     -0.062500
2       -0.041667      0.000000
3       -0.031250      0.000000
4       -0.025000      0.050000
...      ...     ...
95       0.011719     -0.011719
96       0.011598     -0.011598
97       0.011480     -0.011480
98       0.012626     -0.011364
99       0.012500     -0.011250

100 rows × 2 columns
```

Well, for this time, the stubborn strategy seems to prevail.

I will leave the searching for the ground truth to you, the readers.

Exercise

1. **A better strategy**

   Use the 4 by 4 grid, increase the number of iterations, and find out which strategy outperforms the other. Note that you may need to change the frequency the data collector collects data. You are encouraged to use a distribution visualization like the histogram plot to compare the results.

2. **A larger grid**

   Try the simulation on a larger grid and compare the result with the smaller one. Can you try 5 by 5?

Summary

In this chapter, we discussed a new kind of simulation: agent-based simulation (modeling). Agent-based simulation is fascinating because it is capable of generating complex patterns from simple rules that govern local agents' behaviors. It is widely used in computational social science. We also utilized the Mesa Python library to model a multi-agent competition.

CHAPTER 8

Disease Spreading, Simulating COVID-19 Outbreak

Starting from the end of 2019, a regional respiratory disease first identified in Wuhan, China, quickly spread to the whole world. Tens of millions of people got infected and hundreds of thousands of people died. The disease was later named COVID-19 by the World Health Organization. Starting from early 2021, vaccines began to be available, which significantly reduced the death rate for infected people.

As of early 2022, the battle between COVID-19 and humans is still ongoing. In this chapter, we will try to use mathematical models to model and simulate the disease spreading. We will study the very basics of differential equations and run some Python codes to simulate the growth of an epidemic.

Simplifying the Real World

In the real world, disease spreading is a very complex problem. Different diseases have different pathogens: virus, bacteria, or other microorganisms. They have different pathways to invade hosts. For example, the COVID-19 virus mainly spreads through air when infected people cough or speak and susceptible groups breathe in the particles that carry the virus. The virus can also last for quite a long time on surfaces: if another person touches the surface and then touches their nose or eyes, the virus can also invade the new host. Other pathogens can spread through water or food like various kinds of parasites. Certain viruses can also be transmitted through blood like HIV, the cause of AIDS.

© Rongpeng Li and Aiichiro Nakano 2022
R. Li and A. Nakano, *Simulation with Python*, https://doi.org/10.1007/978-1-4842-8185-7_8

The infected population also has huge internal diversity. Take COVID-19, for example; people who are younger with strong immune systems can usually recover without treatment. However, for older people with preexisting conditions, the symptoms can be deadly. Some infected people are more active outdoors, so they can be a source of virus spreading, while other people may choose to stay indoors.

In this chapter, we will try to model disease spreading by focusing on the partition of the population and the simplified interaction between pathogens and the population. The exact details of pathways and biological dynamics of pathogen-host interaction will be omitted.

Here are the main assumptions:

1. The whole population in the world is categorized into three groups: the *susceptible* denoted by S, the *infected* denoted by I, and the *recovered* denoted by R.

   a. The susceptible represents the group who are not currently infected.

   b. The infected represents the group who are currently infected and contagious.

   c. The recovered represents the group who are immune to the disease at a certain point. Note that some versions of the models will use *Removed* instead of *Recovered* to include the deceased population.

2. Group populations are not static, but dynamically changing. For example, susceptible people can get infected and become infected. Depending on the nature of the disease, people may or may not develop immunity. For example, a parasite-caused disease can be recurring if hosts are exposed to the pathogens again after recovery.

3. The model is used to model outbreaks such that many underlined quantities are fixed. For example, the age structure of the whole population is fixed, and the total population remains unchanged as well.

In summary, the most basic structure of the model looks like the following. A susceptible person got infected, then the person recovered, hopefully, from the disease. Figure 8-1 illustrates the relationship.

Figure 8-1. *Relationship between susceptible, infected, and recovered populations*

In addition to this simple trajectory, there may be other trajectories as well which increases the complexity of the system. However, before diving into those ones, let's start with an even simpler model, the SI model: the *susceptible-infected model*.

The SI Model

The SI model doesn't have a *recovered* category; people are either susceptible or infected. A susceptible person can get infected, and an infected person may recover from it. The disease is usually not deadly with a quite low death rate, but it is just not going anywhere. Figure 8-2 shows the bidirectional relationship of the susceptible and infected populations.

Figure 8-2. *The population migration of susceptible and infected populations*

The changes from and to one category to another depend on the interaction between people belonging to each group. Let's use $S(t)$ and $I(t)$ to denote the population of these two groups at timestamp t. How will they change after a timestep, say one hour or one day, whichever unit we prefer to define the modularity in the time domain? I will use day as our time unit as it makes more real-life sense to collect statistics daily rather than hourly.

Imagine a small community; at the very beginning, there are $S(0)$ people who are susceptible and $I(0)$ people who are already infected. Each of the susceptible people has a *chance* to interact with any of the infected people. It is a combination question. If there are five susceptible persons and four infected, then theoretically there are 20 ways for them to interact.

Technically, not every interaction leads to infecting susceptible persons, so there is a ratio. Let's use α to denote such a ratio. The newly infected people will be αSI.

On the other hand, the infected persons will also have a chance to get rid of the infection and become susceptible again. This change is independent of susceptible-infected interaction. Let's assign a ratio β to this process.

In summary, this is how the populations of the two categories evolve in time:

$$S(t+1) = S(t) - \alpha S(t)I(t) + \beta I(t)$$

$$I(t+1) = I(t) - \alpha S(t)I(t) + \beta I(t)$$

These two equations are called difference equations as we are modeling the differences of quantities. A continuous version of the equations is called differential equations; they are defined as follows:

$$\frac{dS}{dt} = -\alpha S(t)I(t) + \beta I(t)$$

$$\frac{dI}{dt} = -\alpha S(t)I(t) + \beta I(t)$$

The differential equations can be solved analytically, but let's focus on the difference equations.

Remember that the total population is fixed, so we can further simplify the two difference equations into one. We use N to denote the total population. The constraint states that for any time t, we have $N = S(t) + I(t)$.

Therefore, we can rewrite the expression of S(t+1) as

$$S(t+1) = S(t) - \alpha S(t)(N - S(t)) + \beta(N - S(t))$$

then

$$S(t+1) = \alpha S(t)^2 + (1 - \alpha N - \beta)S(t) + \beta N$$

It looks straightforward enough. Let's write some code now:

```
N = 1000
beta = 0.01
alpha = 0.001
```

```
Ss = [500]
Is = [500]
Steps = 20
for _ in range(Steps):
    s = Ss[-1]
    s = alpha*s*s + (1-alpha*N-beta)*s + beta*N
    Ss.append(s)
    Is.append(N-s)
```

Let's plot the tracking of the susceptible and the infected populations. Note that we may have float numbers which is inevitable.

```
with plt.xkcd():
    plt.scatter([i for i in range(Steps+1)],Ss, label = 'susceptible')
    plt.scatter([i for i in range(Steps+1)],Is, label = 'infected')
    plt.title("SI model for high contagious disease")
    plt.xlabel("Days")
    plt.ylabel("Sizes of Groups")
    plt.legend()
```

The result in Figure 8-3 shows that we end up with an overwhelmingly infected community.

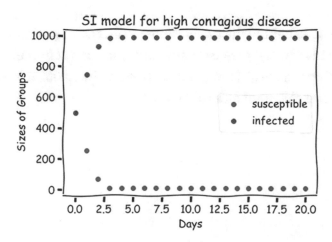

Figure 8-3. *Population evolution for susceptible and infected groups after 20 days*

There are two ways to push the infected population down. We can try two methods. The first way is to limit the transmission between the infected and the susceptible: reduce α; another way is to cure the infected population by increasing β. Let's see how they affect the population evolution curves.

First, let's change α to one-tenth of the original one:

alpha = 0.0001

It looks like we successfully *delayed* the transmission of the disease! Note that I extended the time range to 100 days to see the full picture in Figure 8-4.

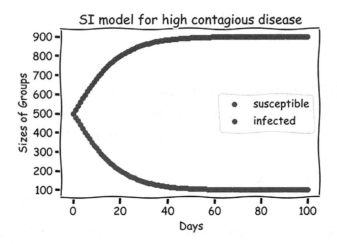

Figure 8-4. *Population evolution*

Well, this is the idea behind the *stay-at-home* or *lockdown* policy. If people limit face-to-face interaction to reduce the transmission rate, the virus will spread much slower.

What if we further reduce α? How about setting α to be 0.00002? You will find that there is no population change at all as in Figure 8-5.

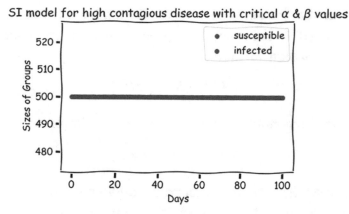

Figure 8-5. *Critical parameters establish equilibrium*

Simple calculation shows that when α and β values are *critical*, the transfer between two populations will reach a balanced state: the number of susceptible people converting to infected people is *exactly* the same as the number of infected people converting to susceptible people.

Exercise

1. What if we further restrict people's interaction? Can you verify that the disease will actually go away?

2. Manipulate the value of β and check its influences on population evolution.

3. Change the initial population of the two groups. If there are only a few infected people at the beginning, will the end state change compared with the more infected people cases? Can you identify the importance of the ratio $\dfrac{\alpha S(0)}{\beta}$?

The SIR Model

Now, let's take one step further to include the *recovered* group. The definition of *recovered* can be further extended later. However, for now, let's first assume that there is only one possible way to get people *recovered*: to get infected, then recover with immunity.

We introduce another variable $R(t)$ to denote the total number of recovered people. It follows the following difference equation. We have a *recovery rate* denoted by γ. People who recover will have *permanent* immunity.

$$R(t+1) = R(t) + \gamma I(t)$$

The restriction of our community population therefore becomes

$$N = S(t) + I(t) + R(t)$$

Let's start with a small γ without any recovered population. What do you expect?

The code is very similar to the one we had earlier, but this time we will explicitly update the three groups:

```python
N = 1000
beta = 0.01
alpha = 0.0001
gamma = 0.0001
Ss = [500]
Is = [500]
Rs = [0]
Steps = 50
for _ in range(Steps):
    s, i, r = Ss[-1], Is[-1], Rs[-1]
    s_next = s - alpha*s*i + beta*i
    i_next = i + alpha*s*i - beta*i - gamma*i
    r_next = r + gamma*i
    Ss.append(s_next)
    Is.append(i_next)
    Rs.append(r_next)

with plt.xkcd():
    plt.scatter([i for i in range(Steps+1)],Ss, label = 'susceptible')
    plt.scatter([i for i in range(Steps+1)],Is, label = 'infected')
    plt.scatter([i for i in range(Steps+1)],Rs, label = 'recovered')
    plt.title(r"SIR model for small $\gamma$")
    plt.xlabel("Days")
    plt.ylabel("Sizes of Groups")
    plt.legend()
```

It looks like after 50 steps, there isn't much increase in the recovered group as shown in Figure 8-6.

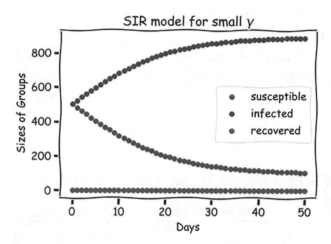

Figure 8-6. *Recovered population stays the same*

Why? Because we are counting on the *natural immunity* which is characterized by the small value of γ.

However, note that people who are immunized will remain so forever; eventually, everyone in the community will be safe. How long will it take? I will leave it to you, but my finding is that it will take more than 20 years for about half of the population, 500, to be immunized. The result is shown in Figure 8-7.

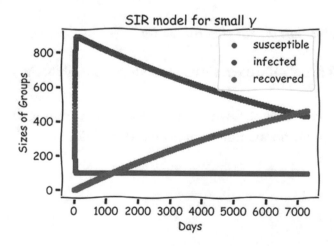

Figure 8-7. *Long march to natural herd immunity*

Now, what can we introduce to the game? The answer is vaccination! If we can convert the susceptible population to the *recovered* state, then the status of so-called *herd immunity* can be reached much faster! Note that the word *recovered* is no longer literally defined now.

How do we do that? Let's say at any point of time, there is about 2% of the susceptible population who are willing to get vaccinated, we may have a much better chance of controlling the disease spreading. Let's call the associated parameter μ.

$$R(t+1) = R(t) + \gamma I(t) + \mu S(t)$$

Let's see how this affects our simulation as shown in Figure 8-8.

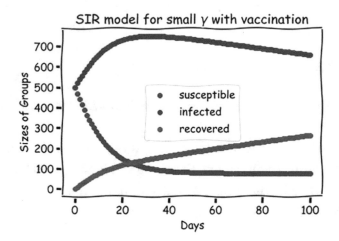

Figure 8-8. *Vaccination boosts the immunity*

Not bad, right? In only 100 days, we have about one-fourth of the whole population immunized.

How about an even higher willingness to get vaccinated among the population? Let's say 5% of the susceptible population want to be vaccinated. The result is very promising in Figure 8-9.

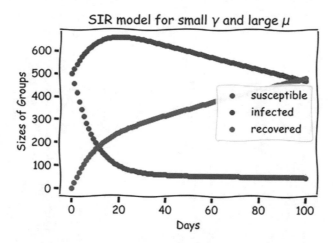

Figure 8-9. *Stronger vaccination will drive faster herd immunity*

The result is even more impressive; we immunized half of the population in 100 days.

Exercise

1. There is a chance that vaccinated people may become susceptible again. Can you model such a phenomenon? How will it affect the herd immunity progress?

2. How will death affect our model? Further divide the *recovered* group to the *real* recovered group and the unfortunate deceased group and explain how the simulation behavior will change.

Summary

In this chapter, we modeled the interaction between different groups during a pandemic outbreak. We simplified the assumptions of the pathogen transmission process and introduced the susceptible-infected (SI) and susceptible-infected-recovered (SIR) models. From the simulation, we can clearly see how different factors influence the virus transmission process and how vaccination can help communities reach herd immunity.

## CHAPTER 9

Misinformation Spreading and Simulations on a Graph

Misinformation has never been so deadly in the age of COVID-19. On social networks like Twitter and Facebook, conspiracy theories about the origin of the virus, the treatment of the virus, and vaccination are rampaging. They often spread in communities and circles and echo with other conspiracy theories about the US presidential elections. Such misinformation and conspiracy theories reinforce each other and form a waterproof *echo chamber*.

Misinformation and disinformation are quite similar. The difference is that disinformation is false information that is spread deliberately to deceive. In other words, disinformation is wrong *on purpose*. Misinformation is a super set of disinformation. The spreader of misinformation may be unaware of the incorrectness or harmfulness of the wrong information. In this chapter, we will study how misinformation spreads with a network/graph setting.

Model the Social Network

We have studied some network-like systems earlier like the state transition of the Markov model and the forest fire spreading model. In the Markov model of poem generation, we treat each word as a node, and each node has a probability to be followed by another one, thus forming a network of words with *directional* edges.

© Rongpeng Li and Aiichiro Nakano 2022
R. Li and A. Nakano, *Simulation with Python*, https://doi.org/10.1007/978-1-4842-8185-7_9

In the forest fire spreading model, each tree is neighbored by four nearest trees on a square grid. Fire can spread from one tree to another with a predefined probability. The network is somewhat homogeneous because they all have four neighbors, except the boundary ones, and no tree is special than another in any way.

In this chapter, we will study *general* networks that can represent arbitrary connectivity of a community. Let's first introduce some terminologies.

So far, I have been using network and graph interchangeably in this chapter. Their definition differences are usually subject to the underlined scientific domains. For example, sometimes people use *links* instead of *edges* in networks, but they essentially represent the same thing. For consistency with other literature, I will use graphs for the following content.

A graph is consistent with *nodes* and *edges*. For example, Figure 9-1 has five nodes and six edges.

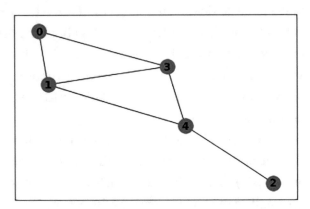

Figure 9-1. *A simple graph with five nodes and six edges*

The graph in Figure 9-1 is also a *connected* graph because you can reach any node to any other by traversing the edges. This is not always true. The graph in Figure 9-2 is a disconnected graph.

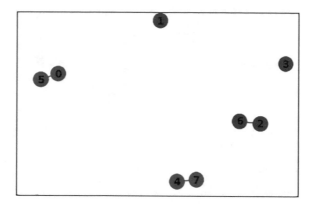

Figure 9-2. *A disconnected graph example*

This graph has five disconnected *clusters* (also called *communities*). They are not connected through edges.

A common misconception is the definition of *subgraph*. Any subset of nodes and edges from one graph will form a subgraph. Those nodes and edges may not be *visually* forming a *cluster*. For example, in the five-cluster graph earlier, node 1 forms a single-node subgraph, while nodes 1, 2, 3, and 6 together with the edge between 2 and 6 also form a four-node subgraph, although a weird one in three visually disconnected clusters.

A graph's edge can also be directional, which makes a graph *directional*. For example, the Twitter following relationship is a directional relationship. You may follow a super star, but the super star is not likely to follow you back. If two Twitter accounts follow each other, then there must be *two* edges between them to represent such a relationship: one from one to the other and the other way around. We call such a graph which allows multiple edges between nodes a *multigraph*. Oftentimes, multigraphs represent directional relationships but not always.

Figure 9-3 is a directional multigraph. The edges are directional, and multiple edges are allowed. For example, there are two edges between nodes 2 and 3. Another interesting edge is the *loop* edge that points to the node itself for nodes 0, 1, and 2. With proper modeling, a loop can represent a tweet's self-retweet or similar actions. Figure 9-3 is a directed graph example.

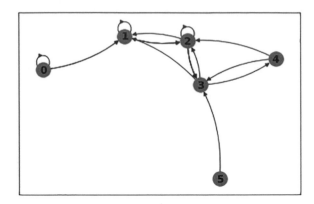

Figure 9-3. *A directed graph with self-loops*

Nodes and edges can also have attributes. For example, nodes can have weights that indicate how influential they are in the graph, while edges' weights can represent how strong the bondings are between two nodes. To model a social network, we need to assign certain attributes to graph elements, either intrinsic or calculated.

Let's define our social network, specifically the Twitter ecosystem, using a graph. Each node represents an account, and each edge represents a following relationship. Information can therefore flow from the followee to the follower through posting tweets.

Think about the properties of a Twitter account. The most important indicator of an account's influence is the number of followers; in our case, it is exactly the number of outgoing edges. In graph theory, it has a name: *out-degree*, the number of outgoing edges. Similarly, the *in-degree* counts the number of incoming edges. The larger the out-degree is, the more accounts on the social network can be potentially influenced.

We want to also borrow some concepts from the previous chapter. We will partition the nodes into three categories, besides the sources of misinformation, like in the *susceptible, infected, and recovered* model. The susceptible are accounts who haven't been exposed to misinformation; they have a probability to be infected if the people they follow are the sources of the misinformation or infected. The infected nodes are like the infected patients in the disease spreading simulation that they actively influence their followers by retweeting and sharing misinformation. The *recovered* nodes are accounts who either intrinsically resist, *R* for both *resistance* and *recovered*, misinformation or recover from misinformation pollution.

In summary, we use the properties in Table 9-1 to characterize a node on the graph.

Table 9-1. *Properties of nodes/accounts in a social network*

Name	Description	Possible Values	Changeable
State	The state of the node	"Source," "Susceptible," "Infected," or "Recovered"	Yes
Influence	How influential the node is, measured by the out-degree	A nonnegative integer	No*
Resistance	The resistance of an account against misinformation	A value between 0 and 1	Yes

The *influence power* is not changeable because our social network is not dynamic. If we allow the follower-followee relationship to change during the simulation, which is much more realistic, then the influence power of a node will change if fewer and fewer accounts follow it.

Now, we have all the static settings laid out. The next step is to define the mechanism that governs the simulation.

Simulate Misinformation Spreading

A simulation starts with a few nodes, likely malicious, beginning spreading misinformation. Their susceptible followers will respond to the misinformation and react. The followers may become infected or stay susceptible. If a follower becomes susceptible, the follower's followers will also be exposed to misinformation and so on and so forth.

At any time, a susceptible node has a chance to recover.

The probabilities in the simulation are also dynamic. For example, if a node is exposed to multiple sources of misinformation, then the chance that they become infected can become very high, while the chance of recovering can be strongly suppressed.

Simple Cases

Let's start with a simple case, in Figure 9-4, with only five nodes to test the accuracy of our code. The graph looks like Figure 9-4. Note that nodes *0* and *1* are following each other.

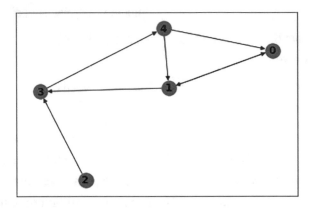

Figure 9-4. *A directed graph with five nodes*

The following is the code to generate the graph:

```
# import networkx as nx
# import matplotlib.pyplot as plt
fig, ax = plt.subplots()
sg = nx.fast_gnp_random_graph(n=5, p=0.2, seed = 3, directed = True)
pos=nx.spring_layout(sg,seed=5)
nx.draw_networkx_nodes(sg, pos, ax=ax)
nx.draw_networkx_labels(sg, pos, ax=ax, font_weight='bold')
nx.draw_networkx_edges(sg, pos, ax=ax, edgelist= sg.edges());
```

Networkx is a powerful Python library to manipulate graphs. Its syntax is quite straightforward. The only non-intuitive method in the preceding code is *fast_gnp_random_graph*. It is a built-in graph generator that, in this example, generates *5* nodes and arbitrarily connects every pair with a probability of *20%*. You can choose to generate a directed graph and set the random seed for reproducibility as well. I choose the name *sg* because it is indeed a *small* graph.

We can check the nodes and edges of the graph by running the following:

```
sg.nodes, sg.edges
```

The results are two nicely ordered iterables:

```
(NodeView((0, 1, 2, 3, 4)),
OutEdgeView([(0, 1), (1, 0), (1, 3), (2, 3), (3, 4), (4, 0), (4, 1)]))
```

We can also check the neighbors of a specific node:

```
list(sg.neighbors(1))
```

For node *1*, the code returns nodes *0* and *3*. Node *4* is not returned because the *neighbors* method only returns the *successors*. In the social network context, it means we are only viewing the followers of node *1*.

To see all neighbors including the followee, we use

```
list(nx.all_neighbors(sg,1))
```

This returns *[0, 4, 0, 3]*; we have duplicates because the relationship between *0* and *1* is *bidirectional*. We can easily use a set operation to deduplicate it.

One last piece of networkx knowledge is the usage of attributes. Each node and edge in a graph can have attributes. For example, the following code will assign a value to node 1 with an attribute name *attr1_1*. This can be very handy to update attributes of the social network accounts.

```
sg.nodes[1]["attr_1"] = "val_1"
```

First, let's define some helpful data structures:

```python
class State(Enum):
    SOURCE = 0
    SUSCEPTIBLE = 1
    INFECTED = 2
    RECOVERED = 3

STATE2COLOR = {
    State.SOURCE: "red",
    State.SUSCEPTIBLE: "grey",
    State.INFECTED: "orange",
    State.RECOVERED: "green"
}
```

We can now initialize the attributes of our simple five-node graph as follows:

```
import numpy as np
np.random.seed(1)
for node in sg.nodes:
    sg.nodes[node]["influence"] = len(list(sg.neighbors(node)))
    if node == 4:
        sg.nodes[node]["state"] = State.SOURCE
        sg.nodes[node]["resistance"] = 0
    else:
        sg.nodes[node]["state"] = State.SUSCEPTIBLE
        sg.nodes[node]["resistance"] = np.random.random()
```

We can now plot the graph with color indicating the initial state of the accounts. As the dictionary *STATE2COLOR* denotes, red means the source of the misinformation. Figure 9-5 indicates the source of misinformation.

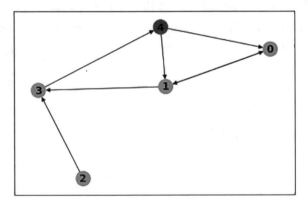

Figure 9-5. *Source of misinformation is in red*

To simulate the simultaneous states updating in one step, we need to

1. Update the states of each node and save the state in a copy of the graph

2. Copy the states to the original graph

3. Repeat steps 1 and 2

Here is the code skeleton for each iteration:

```
for _ in range(5):
    sg_copy = sg.copy()
    for node in sg.nodes:
        update_state(sg, sg_copy, node)
    # copy state
    for node in sg.nodes:
        sg.nodes[node]["state"] = sg_copy.nodes[node]["state"]
```

All the property updating details are in function *update_state*. The logics can be extended further, but here is the first version:

```
def update_state(sg, sg_copy, node):
    # update states in sg_copy to achieve simultaneous updates
    successors = set(sg.neighbors(node))
    predecessors = set(nx.all_neighbors(sg,node)) - successors
    state = sg.nodes[node]["state"]
    if state == State.SOURCE:
        return
    elif state == State.RECOVERED:
        if sg.nodes[node]["resistance"] > np.random.random():
            sg.nodes[node]["resistance"] = min(sg.nodes[node]
            ["resistance"]*2,sg.nodes[node]["resistance"] + np.random.
            random(), 1)
        else:
            sg_copy.nodes[node][state] = State.SUSCEPTIBLE
    elif state == State.SUSCEPTIBLE:
        source_influenced = State.SOURCE in [sg_copy.nodes[pre]["state"]
        for pre in predecessors]
        infected_influenced = State.INFECTED in [sg_copy.nodes[pre]
        ["state"] for pre in predecessors]
        if source_influenced or infected_influenced:
            if sg.nodes[node]["resistance"] < np.random.random():
                sg_copy.nodes[node]["state"] = State.INFECTED
```

```
    elif state == State.INFECTED:
        # infected has a chance to become recovered
        if sg.nodes[node]["resistance"] > np.random.random():
            sg_copy.nodes[node]["state"] = State.RECOVERED
        else:
            sg.nodes[node]["resistance"] = max(sg.nodes[node]
            ["resistance"]/2, sg.nodes[node]["resistance"] - np.random.
            random())
    else:
        print("Unsupported state, exit.")
```

Our logic is based on the observation of accounts' behaviors on social media. The source of the information is always trying to influence the followers. A susceptible person will be infected if their resistance is smaller than a random number.

For an infected person, there is a chance to become recovered by comparing against a random number, but if it fails, the resistance will be halved or reduced by a random number, whichever is larger.

For a recovered person, the resistance will be increased, up to 100% immune, if the resistance is greater than a random number in each round; otherwise, the person will fall back to the susceptible domain.

We already see the initial state, but let's also take note of the resistance numbers:

```
{node: sg.nodes[node]["resistance"] for node in sg.nodes}
```

```
{0: 0.417022004702574,
 1: 0.7203244934421581,
 2: 0.00011437481734488664,
 3: 0.30233257263183977,
 4: None}
```

Next, let's explore the system step by step. Depending on the random number seeds, your results may look different from mine. After four iterations, my network looks like the one in Figure 9-6. The resistance values remain unchanged, but account *0* bought the story pushed by account *4*. Figure 9-6 shows the updates of states.

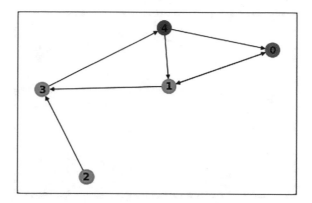

Figure 9-6. *Account 0 is contaminated with misinformation*

Just after another iteration, my graph changes to the following. Account 1, with a relatively high resistance, bought the story, as shown in Figure 9-7.

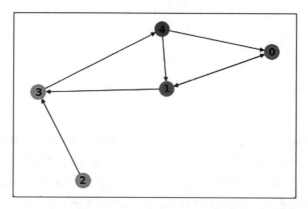

Figure 9-7. *Account 0 recovered, while account 1 bought the story*

After two more iterations, things change again. Figure 9-8 shows that none of account 4's followers believe in it.

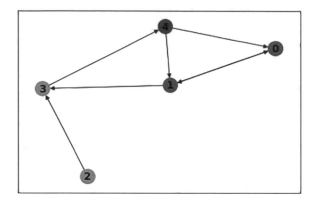

Figure 9-8. *Both accounts 0 and 1 are immune to account 4's misinformation*

The resistance data shows that account *1* is not only recovered but also highly unlikely to buy the misinformation spreader's story anymore.

```
{0: 0.417022004702574,
 1: 0.9184259825270369,
 2: 0.00011437481734488664,
 3: 0.30233257263183977,
 4: None}
```

Such states are likely going to last forever as account *4* has no approach to reach account *3*, unless ads are available. We say that our system is stable.

Let's try a bigger system with ten accounts and a different topology. In this topology, there are much more bidirectional connections which can represent a small community, like a family group or a local community. This topology is represented in Figure 9-9.

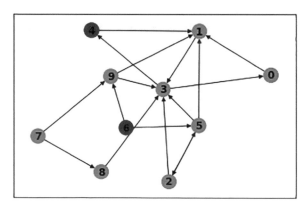

Figure 9-9. *A graph with more bidirected relationships*

I randomly pick accounts *4* and *6* as the sources. After one iteration, two other accounts are *infected* as shown in Figure 9-10.

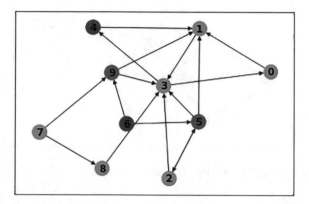

Figure 9-10. *Two followers of the misinformation source got infected*

After four iterations, account *9* is recovered, while account *3* is infected. Figure 9-11 shows the evolution.

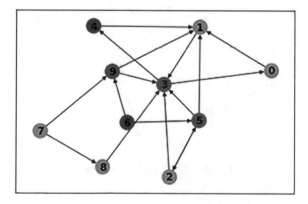

Figure 9-11. *Account 9 recovered, while account 3 got infected*

Continuing the simulation, the stable state of my system looks as in Figure 9-12.

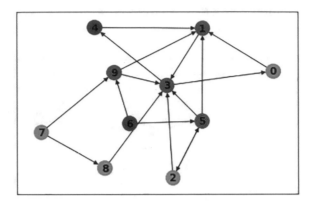

Figure 9-12. *The stable state of the first simulation*

Note that simply changing the random seed initiator can significantly change the final stable state of the graph. Another stable state is presented in Figure 9-13.

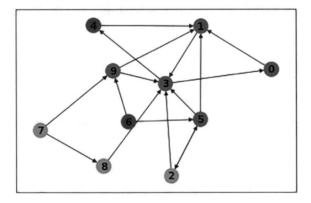

Figure 9-13. *Another stable state with a different random number seed*

Alrighty, let's move on to much bigger graphs.

Misinformation Spreading on Different Networks

The preceding graphs don't actually capture the essence of online social networks. First, they are too small. Second, they don't exhibit the most significant properties of social media networks: only a small portion of accounts have the majority of the followers.

To understand it, let's plot the distribution of the numbers of followers in the network. We need to create a bigger graph using the *fast_gnp_random_graph()* function:

```
fig, ax = plt.subplots()
bg = nx.fast_gnp_random_graph(n=1000, p=0.15, seed = 1, directed = True)
degree_sequence = sorted((d for n, d in bg.out_degree()), reverse=True)
ax.bar(*np.unique(degree_sequence, return_counts=True))
ax.set_title("Degree histogram")
ax.set_xlabel("Degree")
ax.set_ylabel("# of Nodes");
```

The result is presented in Figure 9-14.

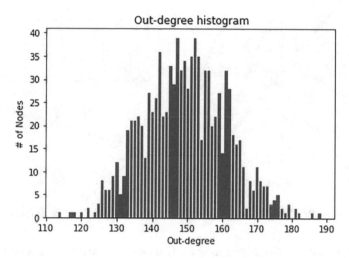

Figure 9-14. *The distribution of the out-degrees of a random graph*

As you can see, the network doesn't have a single, or a handful of, strong influencers. The average number of followers is about 150, and the distribution is almost symmetric. This is not true in real social networks. People don't follow each other randomly with a probability of 15%.

We need to use another random graph generator, the *scale_free_graph()* method. It has many parameters, but we will take the default arguments for simplicity.

Let's take a quick comparison of the ten-node graphs generated by *fast_gnp_random_graph()* and *scale_free_graph()*:

```
fig, axes = plt.subplots(1,2, figsize=(15,6))
G = nx.fast_gnp_random_graph(n=10, p =0.2, seed = 1)
pos=nx.circular_layout(G)
nx.draw(G, with_labels=True, font_weight='bold', pos = pos, ax = axes[0])
```

```
G = nx.scale_free_graph(10)
pos=nx.circular_layout(G)
nx.draw(G, with_labels=True, font_weight='bold', pos = pos, ax = axes[1])
```

The result looks like the one in Figure 9-15. The one on the left is much more centric visually. Well, account 0 *follows* many other accounts, not the other way around though. The result is presented in Figure 9-15.

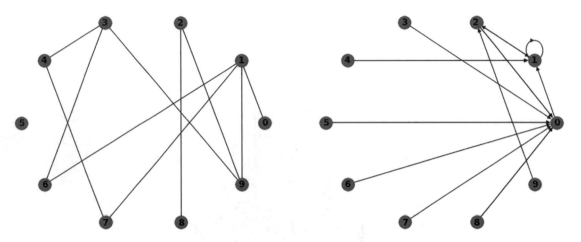

Figure 9-15. *A visual comparison of a random graph and a scale-free graph*

Let's create the same out-degree distribution visualization for a 1000-node scale-free graph. The result is presented in Figure 9-16.

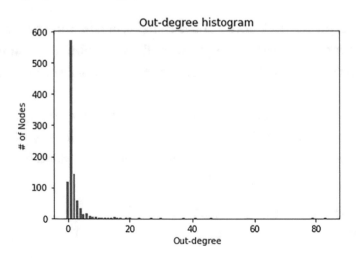

Figure 9-16. *Out-degree distribution for a scale-free graph*

As you can see, there are accounts with more than 80 followers, but the majority of the accounts have only 1 or 2 followers. By controlling the parameters of the *scale_free_ graph* function, you can control the mechanism of the graph generation. The algorithm for generating a scale-free graph is to continuously add new nodes to an existing graph according to a set of preferences. I changed the default parameters to alter the out-degree distribution. For example:

```
fig, ax = plt.subplots()
g = nx.scale_free_graph(1000, alpha = 0.6, beta = 0.39, gamma = 0.01,
seed = 0)
degree_sequence = sorted((d for n, d in g.out_degree()), reverse=True)
ax.bar(*np.unique(degree_sequence, return_counts=True))
ax.set_title("Out-degree histogram")
ax.set_xlabel("Out-degree")
ax.set_ylabel("# of Nodes");
```

The preceding code gives me a more *equal* world that the biggest influencer in the community is not that influential. The largest out-degree in Figure 9-17 is around 30, not 80 as in Figure 9-16.

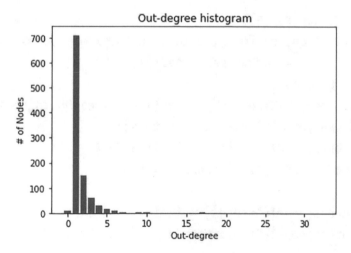

Figure 9-17. *A scale-free graph with a smaller maximum out-degree*

The name *scale-free* comes from the fact that if the network is large enough and you can zoom in to a local small subgraph, you will identify the similar properties and metrics.

We care about the two different cases because misinformation in the second case can spread much faster and dangerously. To quantify that, we need a function to aggregate the numbers of accounts in different state first.

```
from collections import Counter
def count_states(g):
    states = [g.nodes[node]["state"] for node in g.nodes]
    return Counter(states)
```

Alrighty, let's track the spreading of misinformation for both types of graphs. We will randomly generate graphs with 1000 nodes for each case and check how long it takes to reach the stable states. We will also examine the ratios of infected accounts when the stable states are reached.

We will start by setting the top two influential accounts as the sources of misinformation. Note that we can also control the *p* parameter in the *fast_gnp_random_graph* function to control the edge density. It is a crucial parameter because if *p* is very large, then every node is essentially connected with any other node. The misinformation reaches everyone in step one. We will see how it affects the simulation in detail.

First, let me bundle our earlier code into several functions:

```
def initialize(g, top_k = 5):
    tops = sorted(( (n, d) for n, d in g.out_degree()), reverse=True,
                key = lambda pair: pair[1])[:top_k]
    for node in g.nodes:
        g.nodes[node]["influence"] = len(list(g.neighbors(node)))
        if node in [pair[0] for pair in tops]:
            g.nodes[node]["state"] = State.SOURCE
            g.nodes[node]["resistance"] = None
        else:
            g.nodes[node]["state"] = State.SUSCEPTIBLE
            g.nodes[node]["resistance"] = np.random.random()

def simulate(g, steps = 100, top_k = 5):
    initialize(g, top_k)
    res = []
    for _ in range(steps):
        g_copy = g.copy()
```

```
        for node in g.nodes:
            update_state(g, g_copy, node)
        # copy state
        for node in g.nodes:
            g.nodes[node]["state"] = g_copy.nodes[node]["state"]
        res.append(count_states(g))
    return res

def visualize(res):
    steps = range(1, len(res) + 1)
    susceptible = [r.get(State.SUSCEPTIBLE,0) for r in res]
    recovered = [r.get(State.RECOVERED,0) for r in res]
    infected = [r.get(State.INFECTED,0) for r in res]
    fig, ax = plt.subplots()
    ax.plot(steps, susceptible, label="susceptible")
    ax.plot(steps, recovered, label="recovered")
    ax.plot(steps, infected, label="infected")
    plt.legend()
```

The *initialize* method assigns the *SOURCE* state to the *top k* most influential accounts in the graph. Other codes are quite straightforward.

Now, let's run the simulation for 20 steps and collect the statistics. For a normal graph, we use the following code to simulate it.

```
g_normal = nx.fast_gnp_random_graph(n=1000, p=0.002, directed = True)
res = simulate(g_normal, steps = 20,  top_k = 5)
visualize(res)
```

The result shown in Figure 9-18 indicates that the system does tend to reach a stable state fairly quickly, although only 0.2% of all possible edges exist. Go ahead and do the calculation that this is actually a quite large number.

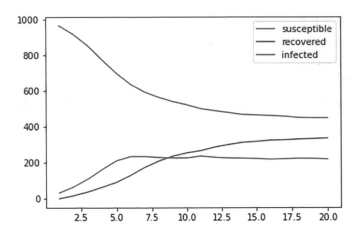

Figure 9-18. *The evolution of populations in a 1000-node random graph*

How about the scale-free graph? Our expectation is that the misinformation spreading should be faster. However, Figure 9-19 doesn't say so.

```
g_scale_free = nx.scale_free_graph(1000, alpha = 0.5, beta = 0.1, gamma =
0.4, delta_out = 0.9)
res = simulate(g_scale_free, steps = 20,  top_k = 5)
visualize(res)
```

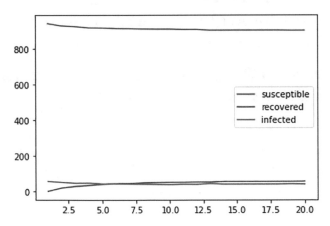

Figure 9-19. *The evolution of populations in a 1000-node scale-free graph*

Clearly, something is off. The system seems stuck in less than five steps. Why? Let's take a look at the most influential account's neighbors:

```
tops = sorted(((n, d) for n, d in g_scale_free.out_degree()), reverse=True,
```

```
key = lambda pair: pair[1])[:5]
```

In my case, account *2* has the most followers:

```
[(2, 15), (18, 14), (6, 12), (11, 12), (32, 10)]
```

Let's examine the neighbors of account *2*. We are mostly interested in the number of their followers:

```
[g_scale_free.out_degree()[k] for k in list(nx.neighbors(g_scale_free,2))]
```

It looks like the majority of them don't have any followers!

```
[2, 0, 0, 0, 1, 3, 1, 0, 9, 0, 0, 0, 0, 0, 0]
```

This is why with a naively created directed scale-free graph, the misinformation spreading is kind of limited to a small *neighborhood* of the sources.

An easy way to fix it is to use an undirected graph. Or significantly increase the top players' influential power in a much larger graph. Unfortunately, the second option crashes my laptop. Please try the first approach on your own.

Lastly, let's check how the *p* parameter in the *fast_gnp_random_graph* method influences the speed of misinformation spreading.

To do that, we need to slightly modify the *simulate* function and make one approximation. When the counting of different states is not changing in the last two iterations, we assume that the system reaches a stable state. Of course, there is a possibility that the situation will change, but that's not very predictable due to random number generation.

The code looks like the following:

```
def simulate(g, steps = 100, top_k = 5):
    initialize(g, top_k)
    res = []
    for _ in range(steps):
        g_copy = g.copy()
        for node in g.nodes:
            update_state(g, g_copy, node)
        # copy state
        for node in g.nodes:
            g.nodes[node]["state"] = g_copy.nodes[node]["state"]
```

```
        if len(res) > 1 and res[-2] == res[-1] == count_states(g):
            return res
        res.append(count_states(g))
    return res

for p in [0.001,0.002, 0.004, 0.01, 0.02, 0.04, 0.08, 0.1, 0.2, 0.4]:
    for _ in range(1000):
        len_res = []
        infected_rate = []
        recovered_rate = []
        g_normal = nx.fast_gnp_random_graph(n=100, p=p, directed = True)
        res = simulate(g_normal, steps = 1000,  top_k = 5)
        len_res.append(len(res))
        infected_rate.append(res[-1][State.INFECTED]/100)
        recovered_rate.append(res[-1][State.RECOVERED]/100)
    print(p, np.mean(len_res), np.mean(infected_rate),
    np.mean(recovered_rate))
```

The result is quite interesting as follows. I am just going to paste the number here:

```
0.001 3.0 0.02 0.02
0.002 4.0 0.03 0.05
0.004 5.0 0.04 0.04
0.01 16.0 0.21 0.12
0.02 10.0 0.2 0.29
0.04 19.0 0.31 0.54
0.08 11.0 0.23 0.64
0.1 17.0 0.4 0.51
0.2 11.0 0.38 0.47
0.4 13.0 0.28 0.6
```

At the beginning, because of the bad connectivity, the simulations stop quite early, and only a small portion of accounts see the misinformation and recover from it. As more and more edges are added to the graph, the stable state takes a longer time to reach with a generally larger size of infected community and recovered community as well.

Exercise

1. Use undirected scale-free graphs to redo the simulation. Check the built-in networkx graph generators to choose the right one.

2. Each account has an *influence* property, which should influence how likely its followers are to accept the misinformation. Introduce a mechanism to address such behavior.

Summary

In this chapter, we discussed another important type of simulation: the simulation on a graph data structure. Specifically, we studied the simulation of misinformation spreading on social media. We introduced basic concepts of graphs and quantified properties to describe graph elements. On top of that, we ran the simulations on different types of graphs and interpreted the behaviors.

Index

A

Absorbing states, 31
Agent class, 116, 119, 120
Agent-based modeling (ABM), 111
Agent-based simulation (ABS), 111, 112
Autonomous agents, 111

B

Bayesian statistics, 47–53
Bell-curve distribution, 8
Beta distribution, 48, 50
Binomial distribution, 48, 49
Bisection method, 16
Bond percolation problem, 79
Breadth-first search, 83

C

calculate_score method, 122
Calculation of Pi
    distribution, 7
    sprinkling grains, 2–9
Cartesian coordinates, 13, 14, 16
Cartesian coordinate system sampling, 14
Central limit theorem (CLT), 8
Circle circumference, 1, 2
clean_limit_orderbook function, 106
Collision detection, 60–64, 74, 75
Community formation on street, 112–115

Conservation of energy, 66
Continuous-time Markov chain, 19
count_threshold variable, 33
COVID-19 virus, 127
Critical occupation probability, 93
Critical probability, 77, 82

D

Dataclass, 42
Data collection, 124
Data schema, 98–102
Debugger PIN, 99
Delta, 62
Depth, 97
Depth-first search, 83
Dictionary keys, 102
Difference equations, 130
Directed graph with self-loops, 142
Directional multigraph, 141
Disconnected graph, 141
Disease spreading, 127, 128, 136
Disinformation, 139
Distribution, 47

E

Eigenstates of Markov Chains, 25–27
Emerging behavior, 111
Exploitation, 41, 44
Exploration, 44

R. Li and A. Nakano, *Simulation with Python*, https://doi.org/10.1007/978-1-4842-8185-7

Printed in the United States
by Baker & Taylor Publisher Services